Robert Allen Campbell

Philosophic Chiromancy

Mysteries of the hand revealed and explained: the art of determining, from an inspection of the hands, the person's temperature, appetites, passions, impulses, aspirations, mental endowments, character and tendencies

Robert Allen Campbell

Philosophic Chiromancy
Mysteries of the hand revealed and explained: the art of determining, from an inspection of the hands, the person's temperature, appetites, passions, impulses, aspirations, mental endowments, character and tendencies

ISBN/EAN: 9783337042226

Printed in Europe, USA, Canada, Australia, Japan

Cover: Foto ©Thomas Meinert / pixelio.de

More available books at **www.hansebooks.com**

PHILOSOPHIC CHIROMANCY.

MYSTERIES

OF

THE HAND

REVEALED AND EXPLAINED:

THE ART OF DETERMINING, FROM AN INSPECTION OF THE HANDS, THE PERSON'S TEMPERAMENT, APPETITES, PASSIONS, IMPULSES, ASPIRATIONS, MENTAL ENDOWMENTS, —CHARACTER AND TENDENCIES.—

By ROBERT ALLEN CAMPBELL.

"He signatureth the hand of every man,
That all the men He hath made may know the man."—JOB.

"As is the mind, so is the form."

ILLUSTRATED.

SAINT LOUIS:
J. W. CAMPBELL & CO.
1879.

Copyrighted 1879, by
ROBERT ALLEN CAMPBELL.

All Rights Reserved.

SLAWSON & PIERROT,
PRINTERS
915 N. Sixth Street,
ST. LOUIS.

BECKTOLD & CO.,
BINDERS,
215 Pine Street,
ST. LOUIS.

PREFACE.

PALMISTRY, as a study and as a practice, is old. The works upon it are numerous — ancient and modern — and of all classes, from the ponderous and scholarly Latin folios of the classic, middle, and dark ages, down to the flash primer of the modern illiterate and pretentious fortune-teller. So this is not a work upon a novel subject.

Many of the facts and explanations here given are of unmeasured antiquity. Some of them are modern — belonging to the present century and generation. A fair proportion are presented here, so far as the author is aware, for the first time. So this lays no claim to being a work presenting only new facts and original thoughts.

Without using "quotation marks," or announcing special credits in detail, the author desires to say that he has culled a fact, selected a truth, and borrowed an illustration whenever and wherever found, provided only that the fact, truth or illustration adopted, was consonant with his experience or confirmed by his observation. The philosophy (as applied to this investigation) underlying the study — the form of presenting the facts and truths — the theory of explanation — the plan of development — and the method of applying the art, together with the rejection of many unproved and disproved conjectures, as well as the announcement of numerous discoveries of his own, and an attempt to recognize the foundation elements of character, rather than collect simply developed results, are the original features claimed by the author.

The author will gratefully acknowledge the reception of any additional facts or principles, or the suggestion (with the reasons) for any correction of statements, theories or principles set forth in the following pages. Any such communications, or any correspondence upon Chiromancy, may be addressed to—

R. A. CAMPBELL,

P. O. Box 2468,

St. Louis, Mo.

CHAPTER I.

ANCIENT PALMISTRY.

CHIROMANCY, or as it is more familiarly known in our day, Palmistry, is one of the oldest of the occult arts. It is now usually thought of, and spoken of, as a cheap delusion; invented, or at least practiced only, by the self-deceived or fraudulent deceivers, to play upon the credulity and empty the pockets of the ignorant, the curious, or the superstitious. In former times, however, palmistry ranked among the learned arts, or was recognized as one of the sacred and peculiar gifts. It was studied and practiced by the philosopher, the priest, and the oracle, among whom it was an esoteric accomplishment and a much prized possession.

Palmistry has been used since the earliest times as a means of reading the past history, and of divining the future fortune and fate of the one presenting the hand. The ablest rulers and the greatest generals have laid their plans or modified them as directed by the palmister. The best and wisest of all classes have reverently held forth their hands to the palmister with mingled emotions of hope and fear. They thus sought to lift the veil of futurity, hoping to catch a glimpse of their general fate, or to see the result of some special undertaking — yet fearing an unwelcome knowledge, by the prediction of an unfortunate, or mayhap a fatal, termination.

Nothing is certainly known concerning the origin of palmistry. Some authors trace it as a gift to mankind by Hermes. Who that mysterious demi-god was, or when or where he lived, and whom he taught we will not now attempt to determine. It is certain, however, that some among the learned of all nations and times have been interested in, and believed in palmistry. Many of them have devoted much time and practice to reading the "mystic lines of man's hand." Thousands of volumes, in Greek, Latin and the modern languages have been written on this department of the "study of mankind."

The author of the book of Job — probably the oldest composition in the world — has put himself on record as a believer in the truth that a man's character is written in his hand. He says: "The palms of the hands He covers over with light." And the same venerable author is yet more emphatic and more explicit in this matter, saying: " He signatureth the hand of every man, that all the men he hath made may know the man."* Palmistry, then, is as old as the days of Job; and Job was contemporary with or preceded Abraham; for the book of Job was an ancient book — probably classic — when Moses wrote Genesis and the Law.

Palmistry was known and practiced in its primitive use of divination, and probably also as a means of reading character, by the ancient Egyptians. Of this ancient Egyptian palmistry we have little or no direct knowledge. We know of it, and what it was — just as we know of Egyptian science, learning, and grandeur — from the frequent allusions to it by the early and classic writers, who, though ancient to us, are, in fact, modern as compared with Egyptian antiquity. These early writers, however, not only allude to Egyptian palmistry, but they make many quotations of its principles and statements; showing that it was a favorite and an occult study with their wise men — both priests and

---

* The best authority sustains these translations, as being better renderings—more faithful to the original—than that given in the authorized version of our Bible.

magicians. It is, therefore, probable that when Moses was "Taught in all the wisdom of the Egyptians" that chiromancy was one of the special accomplishments. And Moses, in his character delineations from the hand, we presume, as far transcended the ordinary Egyptian oracles as his miracles overshadowed their enchantments.

"Daniel was skillful in all wisdom and cunning in knowledge, and understood science." He was familiar with all the learning and philosophy of the Chaldeans, and chiromancy was among the necessary accomplishments of a wise man in Babylon. Daniel was the master of the Chaldean magicians; and through God's illuminating him, he knew the Divine Hand when it appeared on the wall, as well as the meaning of the message written by that hand.

Josephus refers to the art in such a way as to show that he recognized it as of high rank and value.

The Greeks, who borrowed so much from the Egyptians, copied their system of palmistry. To this, however, as to everything else they accepted from others, they added new luster, giving it enhanced attraction, and clothing it in new beauties. They embodied it among their higher esoteric accomplishments, and among their religious rites they gave it special prominence. Homer wrote a complete treatise "On the Lines of the Hand," which, though lost, is frequently referred to by later Greek writers. The probability is that this work was hidden and never found, or that it was destroyed, when chiromancy among the Greeks became a purely esoteric study, imparted only to the favored few, chosen to be instructed in the mysteries of the inner Hermetic Philosophy. In the "inner temple" the instruction was given vocally. Some of this system was written and might be known by all who chose to study it; just as much of masonry in this day may be learned from the Masonic Manuals and other collateral works. Like masonry, however, the vital foundations, the keys by which to unlock the real meaning of Greek palmistry, were not written, or in any way recorded, except on the memories of the initiated. These were kept a living and a sacred secret. They were delivered only in a secure place, duly guarded from all outsiders and eavesdroppers, in the presence of worthy and instructed brethren, by him who had the secret — with the ability and authority to impart the knowledge, to him who had proven himself—and been declared—worthy to receive the instruction; and when imparted it was from the speaking tongue into the attentive ear — and probably in subdued and solemn sentences.

Socrates, Aristotle, Plato, — in fact the greater number of the eminent Greek philosophers and authors — were palmisters.

The Romans imported the art of palmistry from the Greeks, and their priests and augurs were proficient in its practice. In possession of the Romans, however, palmistry lost much of its philosophical character and poetic beauty, and was, by them, applied in a more sensuous and material manner, and to more sordid uses. It was by the Romans again put into writing, its use became more general and it rapidly degenerated in character. The Roman, middle age and dark age palmistrys, mixed up, as it is, with Alchemy, Astronomy and Theology — slumber in a multitude of ponderous volumes, which are seldom studied, and which are usually esteemed as being pregnant with matters curious rather than useful.

Always, however, there have been a few like Paracelsus and Albertus Magnus, who have pursued the study of palmistry — not for gain — but for its own sake. It has in this latter way been kept alive, and handed down to us in its original and developed minutia and purity. Quite a revival of palmistry took place in the seventeenth century. Dr. John Rothman's work was translated into English by Sir George Wharton, and into most of the European languages by different devotees of the art in their various countries, and is the foundation for all the succeeding works upon the subject until the present century.

Modern palmistry has two able exponents — Captain D'Arpentigney and Professor Desbarrolles, both Frenchmen. Captain D'Arpentigney is a scholarly gentleman who has won honorable distinction in the French army. He pursued the study purely as a pastime. He discards all the old traditions of spiritual or astral influence, scouts the idea of divination or fortune-telling, and claims that all he teaches he has learned from his own observation. He has examined many thousands of hands,— carefully noting their peculiarities — but totally ignoring the lines of the palm — and the accompanying character of mind and heart. Professor Desbarrolles, who pursues the study and practice of palmistry as a profession,— in which he is amassing a fortune — attempts to fuse the teachings of the old chiromantists with D'Arpentigney's new system. The Professor boldly asserts and strenuously defends the astrological theory of the planetary influence on mankind through the peculiarities of the hand, which is briefly as follows:

THE ASTRAL THEORY.

It is a fundamental doctrine in palmistry, ancient and modern, that the sun, moon and planets, each exercise a distinct, peculiar and immediate influence upon man. This influence begins at conception and is in peculiar plenitude at birth, the ruling planet at which time exercises such power over the person as to stamp its character upon the entire life. This astral influence extends not only to the whole life in general, but likewise to all its particulars of feeling, thought, and action, in minutia. This astral power largely determines man's years, age, health, fortune, friends — and in short determines his life. All this power is exerted upon man by means of the Astral Light.

THE ASTRAL LIGHT, the palmister tells us, is composed of seven different fluids, just as sunlight is composed of seven different rays of color. These seven fluids emanate from the seven primary planets respectively.

These fluids, separately, and in their combinations, are tempered by the sun and moon. The individual influence of each planet acts upon man by means of the fluid proceeding from it to the man, reaching him through the hand in general, and through the mount bearing its name in particular. The combinations of these fluids, or the aggregate force of them all, working together, is exerted upon man through the hand in general and through the lines of the palm in particular.

The different astral fluids which act upon the hand — separately and conjointly — determine the man's life — recording his past history of disease and fortune as well as deciding his future in these respects. The hand is therefore the reflection of the man; showing his history, present condition and foretelling his future fortune and fate.

The past and the future, the palmister argues, are alike unknown without the historian and the prophet. The future is clearer to the prophet than the past to the historian. The latter must, of course, depend upon the uncertain experience, and upon the still more uncertain traditions of others, who are as imperfect in their senses, and as wavering in their memories as himself. The prophet, however, is especially prepared for his office, and clearly taught by the gods, who see clearly and make exact revelations to their favorite and appreciative subjects. The reflection of man, therefore, painted in his hand by nature and the gods, is clearer and truer than any merely mortal record can be.

It is no more wonderful, then, to read one's future from the hand than it is to tell the past. Each is equally an unmeaning page to him who is ignorant of the language and characters in which the planets write the history and declare the future of the man. These living scriptures, too, are equally plain and certain to him who understands the language in which nature inscribes upon men's hands with uniform clearness, their whole lives — past and present.

To illustrate : it is natural and usual, the palmister remarks, that a general should report to his government the results of his military operations. It is just as usual that he writes out and delivers to each subordinate definite instructions for the direction of the special part required of him. And an able and careful general is quite as explicit in his orders for the movement of his troops, as he is in reporting the manner and result of their achievements. Again the able general, with an overwhelming force, will as a

THE ASTRAL THEORY. 21

whole, be successful in carrying out his design. In some minor matters his plans may be moderately modified, by the opposing forces, or by incident misunderstandings or contentions among his subordinates. In like manner the planets write out their plans upon the hands of each man. They then carry out their decrees, and again upon the hands record the result of their operations. And so man's life and fate is substantially in accordance with their predetermined plans.

The weak yeomanry of the country where a war is carried on, may, by being warned of the general's purposes and plans, and by acting on this information, escape partially the calamity of capture and outrage,— or by heartily coöperating with these plans they may more fully realize the blessings offered by the friendly forces. So the man by knowing the good influences promised, and by being informed of the evils threatened, may court the one to a plenteous consummation, and to a considerable degree escape the worst results of the other.

The result of all this is that man's life depends upon the astral influences, which are constant. The special effect of this influence will depend in each case, upon the peculiar reception of the different astral fluids which reach man in accordance with the individual and combined peculiarities of the mounts and lines of the hand.

Palmisters disclaim absolute fatality in the signs of the hand. These signs, they say, are rather warnings for man's use and benefit. They predict the temptation and the opportunity — the threat of one planet, the favor of the other; but it is still largely in man's power to choose which he will bear or accept; or mayhap make one annul or overcome the other. Hence every man may largely determine his happiness, but cannot to any great degree essentially change his trials or his opportunities.

Such, in short, is the "Astral Theory," which, it is needless to say, the author of this treatise unequivocally discards.

Fortune-telling by the inspection of the hand is universally practiced by the Gipsy women of our day, among whom it is at once a traditional and an exact art. While it is true that these wanderers, like other mortals less traduced, will often "let a dollar blind the eye or quicken the sight" and so read a "bonny fortune" to warm the heart and thus open the purse of their victim; it is still undoubtedly true that two or more experienced Gypsies — when there is no object in deception — will, without any consultation with each other, read substantially the same fortune from the same hand. *Notice.*— I am not claiming for them any ability to foretell the future — or even to recite the past — but simply that they work by uniform and well defined rules, which enables any number of experienced Gipsies — though separated and non-communicating — to see in any certain hand the same peculiarities, and to read from it substantially the same fortune and fate. That is, their art is, when fully understood, an exact one. Whether it is a truthful one, or whether it has in it any elements of truth, as a foundation, is entirely another question.

Palmistry, as a method of fortune-telling, is now practiced by many in Europe and a few in America — among them are numerous scholarly gentlemen and ladies who eloquently and plausibly defend the Astral theory, and claim for their divinations all the certainty of science. Those who practice it are patronized by people in all stations of life, ability and intelligence. Many of undoubted learning, and general ability, occupying respectable and responsible stations in life, gladly and repeatedly consult the palmister, and often make or modify their plans in accordance with his reading, most of whom would scarcely admit full faith in his foretelling.

Napoleon, the Duke of Wellington, Sir Walter Scott, Washington, Webster, Stewart, Vanderbilt, and hosts of others just as able, successful, sensible and celebrated, have consulted palmisters and acted, more or less confidently, upon their predictions and suggestions.

CHAPTER II.

ARGUMENT AND ILLUSTRATION.

THE Astral palmister believes, with Anaxagoras, that man's superiority over the animal kingdom is due to his having hands; that each man's peculiar wisdom, virtue and fortune depend upon the peculiar character of, and are recorded on the lines and mounts of his hands. Many of these Astral palmisters, like their contemporaries, the alchemists and astrologists, have been careful observers. They have discovered and recorded a great number and variety of curious facts connected with the human hand. These facts we can, upon careful confirmation, accept without accepting their false theory of explanation or their method of application. While therefore the mystical influence of the planets upon man, by means of an astral fluid, or otherwise, is entirely repudiated, still the facts recorded by these astral palmisters may be recognized and used just as the earlier astronomers and chemists recognized and used the facts recorded by the astrologers and alchemists.

CHARACTER DETERMINES THE HAND.

Man is not wise because he has hands, but being wise he has hands by which to use that wisdom. A man is not a poet, a musician, an orator, a mechanic, or a laborer as a result of any special features or combinations of lines and mounts in his hands. A man, however, being of a certain character, and in possession of certain powers, has hands revealing that character, and best adapted to use those powers.

The soul is the real man and the body is the material manifestation of the man. The body is, as it were, the clothing and the instrument of the spirit and is developed by the real man for his protection, habitation and use. The body exists and subsists from the spirit, and for its use; and changes naturally, only and solely in obedience to the power and direction of the spirit.

It is true that the body may be changed, mechanically, by outside forces. It may be wounded or worn, distorted or curtailed by accidental objective forces playing upon it. It can be developed only by the spiritual and vital forces working within it. That is, the body may be injured — made *less* a human body by the powers and acts of the outside world. It can be mended or healed, or improvingly developed — made *more* a human body — or a more human body — only by the indwelling spiritual and vital forces; and the form of the indwelling spirit will determine the shape of the living habitation which it generates and sustains.

The poet tells us:

"The mind hath features as the body hath"

He might much more truly have said:

The body hath the features of the mind,
Because the mind hath veiled itself therein.
The outward and the inward worlds are like;
As like as any act is to its thought—
As like as matter can to spirit be.

They correspond in truth as words to thoughts. The soul is constantly developing its body of flesh. Every outline and peculiarity, not the result of some objective opposition or injuring accident, is the result of the character and development of the inner man. The color and contonr of the cheek, the texture and luster of the hair, the depth and light of the eye, every expression of the face, each and all correspond to the features of the soul; and this is true because they are each the incarnation of some affection or thought.

The innocent smile of the child mouth, the restless wanderings of the eye, the curl of the cherry lip, the pure and peaceful face of age, the flushed countenance, the agitated air, all have their meanings, and are each the expression of some inner character or experience.

Our common conversation, in describing or criticizing those we meet shows how fully we all recognize this truth. What more common, or more full of meaning than such expressions as: "a sweet face," "a benevolent countenance," "a friendly air," "a sympathizing look," "a gracious demeanor," "a stiff upper lip," "a hard mouth," "stiff-necked," "thin-skinned," "long-headed," "close-fisted," "open-handed," and so on indefinitely? Every one of these is a literal description of the fleshly body or its action, and every one of them is also a vivid description of the character incarnated in that body; and they are equally true whether as applied to the body or spirit. This is so clearly seen — though not always understood — that the use of these and kindred expressions does not call to our mind the lineaments of the body described, but presents to our imaginations the mental or moral character of the person mentioned.

The body is a representation — a revelation if you will — of the man and a record of his life. Every one, all the life long, is constantly incarnating desires, thoughts and acts in fleshly lineaments, into quality and form, into color and expression. The affections — good and bad, the thoughts — true and false, the acts — virtuous and vicious — growing out of these affections and thoughts, are all plainly written out in the body. The reader, only, is wanting. The page is open, the characters are distinct. The record is indelible. No spiritual chemistry can ever fully erase these eternal histories in the "book of life." The book is clear, exact, and fully posted up to date; some of its characters are known; some of the pages can be translated with tolerable accuracy; some are imperfectly understood; many are as yet obscure; and many are totally unintelligible. We wait the seer to interpret fully the meaning of all the pages. Will he ever come, and if so when?

The trinity of human essentials, without any one of which humanity could not exist, are the will, the understanding, and the action. These are manifested in the affections, the intellect and the life; in the desires, the plans and the works. Man might be endowed with affection, and, hence, with desires and emotions, but could never know, much less use them, without intellect. He might be endowed with intellect, and, hence, with thought, possibly with reason and plan; but he could not know himself — much less any other — in short would not be human without action — and the hands are the organs of action. The affections might warm the intellect and incite the thought, and the intellect might embody the affections in the truest and clearest plans, but without manifesting these affections and thoughts there would be no humanity — and the hands are the organs of manifestation.

The hand is the immediate servant of the will, obeying its orders as planned and directed by the intellect. The hand is the promptest of servants, moving when commanded, and instantly ceasing to act when the will through the intellect ceases to order. As there is no speech without thought, so there is no action of the hand without orders. The will desires, the intellect plans, the hand executes, and one is as essential to humanity as the other. Pure desires and clear thoughts are not known until ultimated, and the hand is the executive of the man.

Without hands humanity might be a latent warmth — not developed, a light not shining, a tone not sounded. Without hands man might be, perhaps, an impulse, possibly a thought, certainly not a fact. The trinity then, affection, thought, action — heart, brain, hand — is each one equally essential to humanity. Without either one of them there could be no humanity, much less any progress of humanity.

THE HAND REPRESENTS THE MAN.

Anatomists have not yet determined the physical home of the affections. The brain, the assumed habitation of the intellect, can not be examined while the master of the house is at home; and a dead brain is certainly a dim and darkened page of indistinct images from which to read — or attempt to read — the living character of the shining intellect. The other member of the human trinity — the action — resides in the hand, and the hand may be seen and studied in life. Not only so, but, aside from its mere anatomy, the hand can be best seen and studied in life.

And further the hand is most expressive when it is most the active agent of the warmest affection and the clearest thought.

It may be questioned whether it is correct to speak of man's affections as located in the heart; or whether the brain is the exclusive seat of intelligence; but there is no doubt that in literature, sacred and profane, prose and poetry, and in speech, classic and provincial, the hand is recognized as representing the whole powers of the man. Poets and prophets have perceived this truth. The intuitive men of all ages have recognized the truth when presented to them. There is no suggestion of any manual action, but unmistakable reference to the conduct, when the poet says:

> "Still in thy right hand carry gentle peace,
> To silence envious tongues,"

Thousands of times in the Bible the hand is used to represent all the powers of the hand. It is so used in every classic, and in nearly every sacred and standard writing of every age and people. No one mistakes the meaning when it is said: "His hand was against every man, and every man's hand was against him." "He ruled them with a heavy hand." "He held him with an iron hand." No woman was ever so ignorant of this truth as to think of any surgical operation when one of the sterner sex asked for a bestowal of her hand.

THE HAND IN DETAIL REPRESENTS THE MIND IN MINUTIA.

Now the hand not only represents the whole man in the way above referred to, but also in a much more marvelous and detailed way. In short the hand is a true index of the mind in minutia. This index is clear, full and distinct. There is no pretense, however, that this index is fully understood, or that it can in all cases be easily read. We can read the character from the hand just so far as we understand the mind and its laws, affection and impulse and their laws, and also know how they are delineated in the hand. With these knowledges we are in possession of the elements from which, and by which, to read the character.

The problem is, from the hand to find the physical peculiarities, the mental idiosyncrasies, the impulses and affections — in short the abilities, aspirations, and opportunities — and from these to deduce the resulting life. This cannot be done easily or perfectly. The only claim is that a good beginning has been made and considerable progress has been accomplished.

Just here the very proper and pertinent question may be asked, " Is there any reason why the hand should index the mind ?" The simple answer is, there is no known *a priori* reason why the hand should index the mind, any more than there is a reason why the sense of touch should be connected with the nerves rather than with the blood-vessels. It is only known as a fact, learned from observvation and experience. Having the statement of this indexing once made, however, we find innumerable facts and abundant illustrations to confirm the truth.

FACTS AND ILLUSTRATIONS.

There is nothing in nature, and, therefore, cannot be in art, which can be successfully compared to the hand in strength and mobility, or in beauty and usefulness. The accuracy and perfect proportion of the bony sleleton of the hand; its muscles, so intricate, and yet so perfectly adjusted, with their wonderful interlacings; its unravelable network of nerves — sensational, volitional and sympathetic; its skin, at once the strongest and most sensitive on the body; its corpuscles of touch, so completely covering some parts of the surface, responding to the lightest pressure, and yet so guarded that only violence can injure them — all these parts and others that might be mentioned,— each so perfect in itself and in its separate function, and still so exquisitely adapted to harmonious and concurrent action, make the human hand at once, the most intricate and symmetrical, as well as the most useful, expressive and beautiful feature of the human body.

TOUCH.

It is said that seeing is believing. But whenever sight is doubted we confirm the fact by touch. So we may without fear of question assert, that if seeing is believing, then, touching is knowing. And touch is most sensitive and exquisite, as well as most delicate and available in the hand.

True, the nerves of sensation are common to the entire surface of the body. These nerves of sensation, however, cognize but two qualities — pressure and temperature. They give but two conceptions — pleasure and pain; the one for our enjoyment, the other for our protection. The nerves of touch are endowed with the superior function of giving conceptions of form, size and locality. All these qualities learned by touch are given through the hand, and almost exclusively through "the eyes of the hand"— the finger-tips.* The touch corpuscles, it is true, are found on the ball of the great toe, on the heel, on the lips, and on the edges of the tongue. But, except in rare cases of special development, the touch corpuscles found in those localities are like those in the hands of infants — rudimentary, and their aggregate number, in ordinary cases, will not equal those found on the tip of one finger.†

The blind reading from raised letters, and in some cases distinguishing the color of fabrics, is a familiar illustration of the possibilies of the sense of touch.

---

* The total independence of the nerves of touch and the nerves of sensation is seen in the many instances of persons acute in one respect and dull in the other. Lepers, who are often delicate in their sense of touch, and expert in the use of their hands, are not sensible to heat or pressure — even when the hand is crushed or destroyed by fire.

† A very novel and pretty experiment is to place the tip of the first finger in the ear — or in both ears. There will first be a buzzing sound, then a perfectly distinct but irregular crackling sound. The finger of another person will produce a different sound — and the irregularities of the crepitations will be modified; that is each person will produce a sound characteristic of the individual owning the finger. Some are so sensitive, as to be able, in this way, to distinguish the sex, age, temperament and somewhat of the condition of health.

Sir Charles Bell has written a book on the hand, which is standard authority, alike with the anatomist, the mechanician, the artist and the theologian. He says: "We ought to define the hand as belonging exclusively to man; corresponding in sensibility and motion with that intelligence which converts the being who is weakest in natural defense, to ruler over animate and inanimate nature." He quotes from Ray, saying:

"Some animals have horns, some have hoofs, some teeth, some talons, some claws, some spurs, some beaks; man hath none of all these, but is weak and feeble, and sent unarmed into the world. Why? A hand with reason to use it supplies the place of all these."

It were truer if he had said: reason, with hands by which to use it is incomparably above all these.

THE HAND AS A MACHINE.

The human hand is the most perfect machine in existence. Examine any instrument, any piece of mechanism, simple or intricate, and notice the limitations and the imperfections. Contrast these with the universality and superiority of the hand. See how hap pily the different proportions and properties of all instrumentalities are combined in the hand. Or rather notice how, even the most perfect mechanism does only one or a few of the innumerable things done by the hand.

In the hand the sensibility to touch and temperature is united with a facility in the joints of unfolding, grasping and moving in every possible degree and direction, without abruptness or angularity, and in a manner and with a varied force inimitable by any artifice of joints and levers. Attention to our most common manipulations will show how the divisions into fingers adapt the hand to an innumerable variety of uses otherwise impossible.

Not quite so obvious, at first sight, perhaps, but just as clearly true, upon careful examination, is the fact, that upon the length and strength, proportion and mobility of the thumb depends the power of the hand. The large fleshy ball formed by the muscles of the thumb, which gives it strength, is one of the distinguishing characteristics of the strong hand.

The hand can wield the sledge of the miner, or draw the finest and fairest line for the engraver. It will for the sailor splice the cable of the Great Eastern, or for the engineer stretch the spider thread across the field of the telescope. It may be trained to remain motionless in one position, or hold firm in one grasp for hours, while for the musician it will strike nearly a thousand notes a minute.

THE HAND AS A SYMBOL.

Moses and Daniel have been referred to as understanding the hand. The former tells us that "Israel went out with a high hand," "Jehovah led us forth with a mighty hand." In his last great speech to the assembled hosts of Israel, gathered about him in the plain, east of the Jordan, he rehearsed to them the laws, saying: "Thou shalt bind them as a sign upon thine hand, and they shall be as frontlets between thine eyes." That is, let the laws be a sign for your hand — a guide to your life — put them in practice by doing them; and then they shall be frontlets — bright and beautiful — attractive and luminous — before your perception.

John tells us, in the Apocalypse, that in the heavens he saw a great multitude * * * clothed in white, and with palms in their hands. The white robes are often referred to as emblems of innocence, purity, virtue, intelligence in divine truths. The palms in the hands — not so often explained — mean the hands working the works of peace, an active life, not controlled by authority, but the outgrowth of pure affection.

The false beast is represented as marking his subjects in the foreheads and in the hands — that is they exhibit themselves as false thinkers and impure livers — ignorance and sin. David, the poet-king of Israel, speaks of the man with "clean hands and a pure heart." The hands are clean because the heart is pure; and they could not be really clean doing the work of an impure heart.

The unwilling and weak Pilate washed his hands of the greatest crime ever committed against the Divine Humanity. Jesus cured diseases and blessed little children by touch of the hand.

Jacob Bœhm, the German seer, says: "The hands signify God's omnipotence, for as God in nature can change all things, and make of them what he pleases, so man, also, can with his hands, change all material things, and change them as he pleases. He rules with his hands the operations of nature, and so they very well signify the omnipotence of God."

Swedenborg, in his Divine Philosophy,

says: "The potency of the whole man, being determined chiefly to the hands * * * therefore, in the Word, the hands signify power, and the right hand superior power."

The grand old observer, philosopher and skeptic, Montaigne, pays a deserving tribute to the hand. In speaking of its uses and possibilities, he says:

"With the hand we require, promise, call, pray, dismiss, threaten, supplicate, deny, refuse, admire, interrogate, number, confess, repent; express fear, confusion, confidence, doubt. Instruct, command, incite, encourage, swear, testify, accuse, condemn, absolve, abuse, despise, defy, provoke, flatter, applaud, bless, submit, mock, reconcile, recommend, exact, entertain, congratulate, complain, despair, grieve, wonder, exclaim, and—what not. And all this with a variety and multiplication emulating speech. With the hand we invite, welcome, honor, demand, rejoice, reject, lament, caress, rebuke, give the lie, inquire, accuse, threaten."

It should be remembered, too, that while the hand can and does express these various thoughts, that it does so in a natural, and, therefore, in a universal language. Speech is understood only by those using the language of that speech; but the expression of the hand is common to and understood by humanity.

SHAKING HANDS.

Every one of ordinary perception has been more or less interested in noticing the different ways in which people shake hands. There is more of individuality exhibited in the performance of this common ceremony of social courtesy than in any other unstudied action of ordinary life. All have experienced the numberless and diverse sensations which are received through this customary method of greeting. Comparatively few, perhaps, have fully analyzed the accompanying emotions or connected them clearly with the subtle sources.

One in this salutation seizes the hand with a hard, cruel grip, and tosses it off with a spasm of turbulent energy that leaves the other physically pained and mentally discomfited. Another lazily extends an inert palm, and with a weak, listless touch makes pretense of conforming to the conventional requirements of the occasion, but with a dead apathy and carelessness which at once disappoints and exasperates a more earnest nature. What happens when two such persons meet is not known; perhaps because neither have the sensations to feel, the perception to notice, or the energy to record, the negative nature of the impression. A not uncommon character is the selfishly receptive absorbant, who holds out a willing hand, expectantly still, to receive whatever greeting is bestowed, but which never once offers a generous pressure or responds to a hearty clasp. Then there is the affected reaching out of the gingerly finger tips, as if to say, I graciously condescend to a common custom — or to an inferior person — but a touch is all I bestow or allow. After meeting these, or any one of numerous other equally repellant types, how gladly the noble nature meets the firm, hearty clasp of a morally magnetic hand, all sensitive of reception, and bounding in generous strength of health and heart which imparts a thrill of kindly kinship and instantly puts the two *en rapport* with the best characteristics of each other, and so brings them into comradeship with the rich personality of all that is noblest in humanity. How full of meaning the remark of one lady to another, "I drew courage and comfort from the very shake of your hand when I first met you." Contrast this with the "fishy hand" of Uriah Heep, whose irritating touch David Copperfield felt forced to wipe off with his handkerchief, it was so vilely odorous of deceit, selfishness and treachery.

THE HAND IN ART.

Poets and painters, sculptors and musicians, have immortalized the hand, and the hand in turn has been the instrumentality through and by which they have immortalized themselves. Job and David, Moses and John, Homer and Hesiod, Shakespeare and Goethe, Milton and Dante, Browning and Emerson have written or sung of the hand.

The Egyptian and Grecian sculptors, the one symbolic, the other representative, have given us innumerable and characteristic hands full of meaning. The painting of human hands by Raphael and Corregio, by Durer and Rubens, by Vandyke and Rembrandt are full of human history. A master's power is shown in every prominent hand delineated by these wonderful men. They displayed the true artistic genius by which they saw the truth, and so, without the dull and imperfect plodding of sensuous experience, or the slow process of deduction, they were enabled, by the inner light, to give the appropriate hand to each great character. And with them, as with all seers, the poet is first to perceive and state the advanced truths. The scientist then comes along and confirms while the logician demonstrates its certainty, and mankind accept as they have ability. The poet lights on the mountain peaks of clear truths, the scientist and logician build connecting highways upon which the masses may travel. The musician not only must needs use his own hand to write out his score when invented, but he depends almost exclusively on the hands of many others, as the means of vitalizing these notes, until their rendition thrills the thousands into an ecstacy harmonious with his own delight.

HOW WE USE THE HAND.

The hand and its work is everywhere. Behind the glass, which fate holds up before us, imagination dimly pictures the shadow of a hand. We are led, we depart or remain, we meet or we do not meet, as the unseen hand determines.

To us, as to the Egyptians, the hand is an emblem of strength. To us, as to the Chaldeans, it is an emblem of invincible power. The king, midst his revelry and feasting, started back aghast, sobered and trembling, at the hand as it wrote on the wall; the writing, which was not understood, surprised him; but the hand, he knew, meant power, and hence struck him with terror. To us, as to the Romans, the hand is an emblem of fidelity. Transitory matters are discussed, exhortations are delivered and minor bargains are made by the tongue; history is recorded, deep reasoning carried on, intricate calculations made and real estate conveyed by the hand. Our ancestors swore by the hand, and we testify uplifting the hand. Men and women are married clasping hands. Friends salute by the hand. Favor, respect and affection are manifested by pressing, and still more by kissing, the hand.

DIFFERING HANDS.

What a difference in hands. Look at the little innocent baby fingers, rosy and clinging —the quick, eager hands of childhood—the restless, busy hands of youth—the dainty, delicate hand of woman, warm with its fluttering pulsations—the firm hand of manhood, strong to strike and tender to caress—the feeble and uncertain hand of age—the cold, dead hands, folded in rest.

What a difference in the same hand, under a change of circumstances! That hand which is strongest for work, which holds more firmly than fetters the offending culprit, or strikes to death the opposing enemy, may still be the most delicate to soothe, the most congenial to quiet the fevered friend; it may, by its kindly pressure, and tender touch, express more eloquently than words, the deepest sympathy in the death-chamber, and may, by its love foldings, impart more confidence than the uttered vows at the nuptial altar.

The hands are always true to the life, and change as the life changes in growth, quality and decay. They are the true index of the inner man, for his daily life has incarnated itself in them. Every desire and the thought in which it is embodied, thrills instantly from the soul, through all the nerves and fibres of the hands and leaves its impress upon them. When warm palm meets warm palm, in the grasp of friendship, or in the clasp of love, it is the soul of the one greeting the soul of the other.

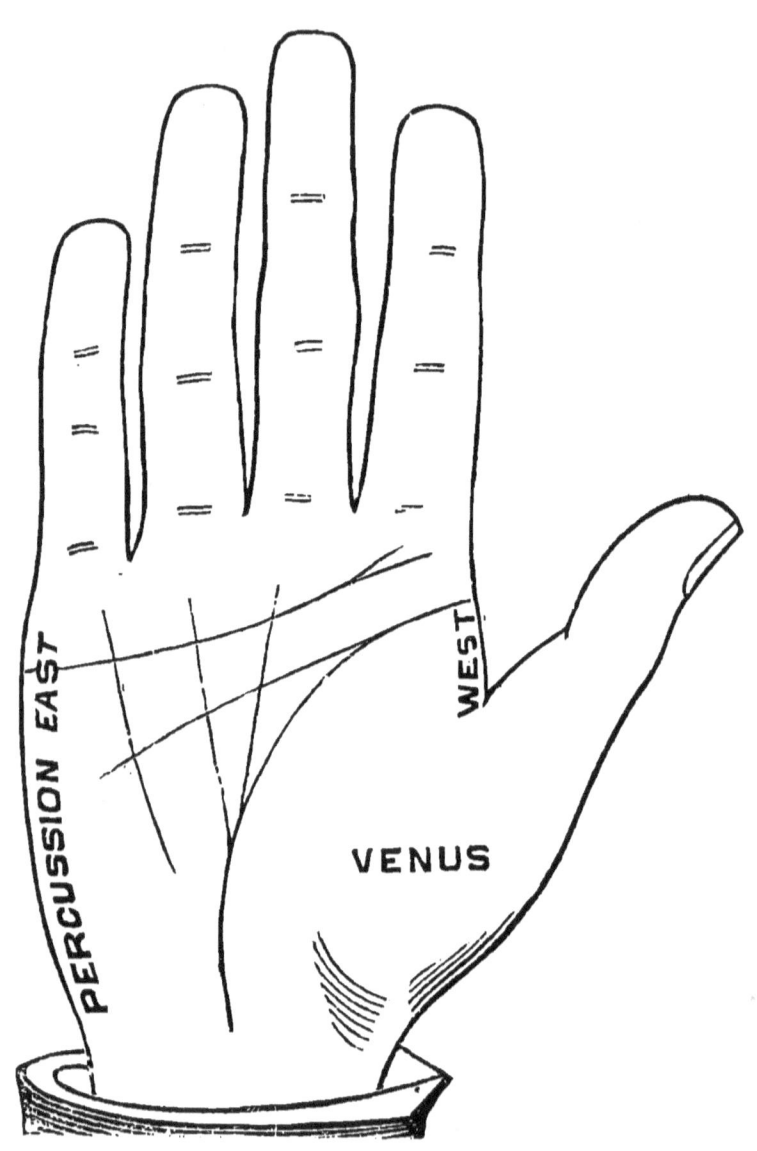

THE HAND IN OUTLINE.

CHAPTER III.

THE HAND IN GENERAL.

HANDS differ indefinitely in size, ranging from the extreme of large to small. This variation extends to each of the three dimensions; so that hands may be anywhere from long to short, from broad to narrow and from thick to thin.

Hands may be of any condition from fleshy to lean. If fleshy they may be plump or flabby. If lean they may be trim and smooth or skinny and wrinkled.

Hands, again, are of almost infinite variety as to being hard, firm, yielding, soft or plastic; elastic or inert; rigid or supple; stiff or flexible; nervous or passive; muscular, sinewy or neither; electric, magnetic or negative; dry, normal, damp or moist; hot, warm, normal, cold or clammy.

The skin of the hand is of innumerable variations and combinations of thickness, texture, quality, sensitiveness, and color.

These differences of the hand in general also apply to the palm as a principal division of the hand, and some of them to the thumb and fingers individually.

It is well known that no two faces are alike, in fact, that no single face is so perfectly balanced that one side is an exact duplicate of the other side. It is just as true that no two persons have hands alike, and just as certain that no pair of hands are exact duplicates. The differences to be found in that pair of hands which are most alike are neither few nor doubtful. It requires no expert to see the variations. Any pair of hands will exhibit marked differences, which will, when pointed out, be readily recognized by any one of ordinary perception. Usually the hands are of different size and vary in many of the points mentioned above. The fingers are often — generally — of different comparative lengths and exhibit other divergent peculiarities. A slight examination of any pair of hands will show that even the principal lines are not exactly alike in the right and left palms. A careful examination will usually show that no single line is exactly like its fellow in the other hand.

Usually the variations in a pair of hands are tangible as well as visible, so that even a blind man can, with his finger ends, note many differences in that pair of hands which are most alike.

The difference between the two hands must be carefully noted, and the meaning and value of the variation should be kept constantly in mind while deducing the person's character.*

The Right Hand points out the direction which the individual is traveling, and the progress made in the modification of original tendencies and abilities into actual character.

The Left Hand indexes the person's natural inclinations and peculiarities, which in a greater or less degree have been modified in the direction shown by the right hand.

In case of "left-handed" people this rule is reversed. In short, the passive hand exhibits the character from which the person is growing; while the active hand indexes the character as developed.

---

* The ancient palmisters teach that if the lines are equally fair in both hands they show that the person resembles the father as to physical form, and is like the mother in mental and moral endowments. The right hand being the clearer and fairer shows that the person resembles the father in physique temper and mind; this resemblance increases as the right hand is fairer and clearer than the left. The left hand exhibiting the fairer lines asserts the person to be like the mother physically, mentally and morally, the more so as the left hand is manifestly clearer than the right.

Divisions of the Hand.—The hand is made up of three essential parts — the palm, the thumb, and the fingers — each of which indexes essential elements in the character and life.

In speaking of the hand, palm or fingers, *up* is towards the finger-tips, and *down* is towards the wrist. *East* is the edge of the hand bearing the thumb, and *west* is the edge bearing the little finger.

The Palm indexes the physical strength, endurance, activity and temperament. It is, also, to a great extent, a bulletin of the health, past and present: and, hence, in some measure, shadows forth the future in this respect. The palm shows the animal appetites and inclinations; the instinctive desires, affinities and repulsions; the sensuous tendencies, aptitudes and impulses; all these in their various combinations of strength and intensity. As the palm dominates over the fingers it shows a preponderance of the animal over the man; as it is extremely hard, especially if horny, it attests approaching brutishness; as it is extremely small it shows lack of muscular strength; as it is extremely soft it indexes lack of endurance and an extreme impressionability. The thick palm shows strength; the broad palm, endurance.

The Ideal Palm is of fair size, in due proportion and condition to harmonize with the person in stature and flesh. It is trim, well rounded, firmly elastic, pliant without being weakly flexible, clearly and evenly colored, moderately and regularly warm, dry without being parched. The skin is soft and flexible without being velvety or plastic, smooth but not glossy. The touch is delicate, kindly soothing, invitingly clinging. The mounts and lines well defined and favorable. Such a palm will herald the perfection of strength, health, endurance, activity and sensibility.

In general terms the lower part of the palm shadows forth the animal strength and instincts; the middle portion shows the power and quality of the brain and nerves; and the upper part indicates the force and character of the emotions. From the comparative firmness of the palm is learned the person's power of physical endurance.

The indications of the palm in minutia are fully discussed under the subsequent sub-headings of this chapter, and in the chapters treating of the mounts and lines of the hand.

Large Hands are the hands that do or work; that naturally, patiently, lovingly put forth manipulating activity. The person with large hands naturally executes his plans; acts out his impulses; materializes his thoughts. Large hands belong to him who naturally finishes one thing before beginning another; to him who carries out his own plans, unless judgment or necessity leads him to employ an assistant or substitute; to him who does not consider his work complete until the thought or feeling is incarnated into action. Large hands are characterized by completeness in the performance rather than by the fertility of theories. They indicate a mastery of what is undertaken, rather than a wide range of abilities.

The Long Hands indicate an appreciation, love and performance of details; a care for, and an ability in the minutia of one's profession. They show persons who will know many details about whatever interests them. (See "*Long Fingers.*")

Small Hands show the man who plans great things, who aspires after the colossal, who sees the result to be attained and the general plan by which to accomplish his ends; who readily states his views in general terms, but who rarely of his own accord goes into details; who is satisfied with completing the plan, and naturally calls upon his larger handed neighbor to put in the minutia, and to finish that part of the work requiring routine, plodding and muscular endurance. Small hands like light work, dainty work; work not tied down to rule and minutia; they delight in work which requires grace rather than exactness, activity rather than continuity, and work in which invention and care are constant elements. (See "*Short Fingers.*")

The Slim Hands, warm and dry, show activity, moderate muscular power, and usually accompany a kindly disposition. This hand, lean, sinewy, and dry, shows little muscular power, nervous irritation, and, hence, may mean — depending on other characteristics — irritable temper, cowardice, or quarrelsomeness. The slim hand, soft, indicates a weak physique, love of ease; and if it is also cold or damp or moist, bodily weakness and inactivity are more fully indicated.

Minutia, finish, elegance, work, belong to large hands. Magnitude, grace, generalities, are the characteristics of small hands. Persons with small hands see the whole, the mass, and work for the grand effect, and hence with a long, free, graceful stroke and with independent, rapid motion. The person with large hands sees the parts, the factors, and works with an eye to the perfection of each one, with an exact and calculated stroke and a careful, steady motion.

The medium-sized hand, the one in fair proportion with the body, is the one that will naturally do, or delegate the doing, as judgment or necessity may designate as best.

James B. Eads, who originated the great tubular steel bridge over the Mississippi, at St. Louis, and who secured the aid of capitalists to build it, has very small hands.

Henry Flad, who worked out the details of construction, and who calculated the details of strain and tension, has very large and very effective hands. The former conceived the grand idea, and, both as an engineer and as an organizer, dealt in comprehensive statements made up of golden generalities, while the latter filled these general plans full of the needed sinews and nerves of detail.

Abraham Lincoln, who was peculiar in the matter of giving personal attention to many minor matters, usually delegated to subordinates, had very long hands. Jay Gould, who forms immense plans, who aims at grand effects, but who does all his work through subordinates, has small and short hands.

Redouté, the illustrious French flower painter, who is especially celebrated for the wonderful detail, minute manipulation, and elegant and exact finish of his pictures, has very large, long hands. Corot, on the other hand, who paints with no attempt at detail or elegance of finish, rather avoiding both, but who aims at the grand effect which many can feel, but which few can see, and fewer understand, has very small hands. The Greeks always associated beauty and strength, demanding a living force great enough to control itself in grand repose. They founded only small States, where all took part in making and executing the laws. They worshiped deities with well-defined and clearly limited characteristics. Their monuments and statuary are unapproachable in perfection of finish, elegance and beauty, but they are all of limited dimensions. The model Greek hand, as shown in the statuary ideals by their best sculptors, is large, with a moderately thick palm and a prominent thumb. The fingers are of medium length, strong, smooth and tapering with mixed oval and square phalanges.

The pyramids and monoliths of Egypt, and the temples of India — as noted for their magnitude, grandeur and sublimity as are the Greek works of art for their finish, elegance and beauty — were planned and their construction superintended by a people celebrated as having the smallest and most delicate hands in the world. The ideal hand of these races — as seen in the contemporary sculpture with which their vast works are usually adorned, as well as shown by the mummies, which were of the ruling classes — are small, of medium width, having short, smooth, tapering fingers, with square and spatulous ends.

The Hard Hand will indicate one who easily puts forth continued action; one who is enduring at physical effort; who delights in energetic activity. The hard hand with elasticity also, not only expends muscular strength and puts forth continuous activity, but is unhappy if denied that necessary privilege.

The Elastic Hand which may also be called the sinewy hand, although the former is the more truthful term, is capable of, and loves, rapid skillful activity. It is characterized by energy rather than by endurance. Persons with an elastic hand are capable of massing much power for short periods of time; capable of expending — under excitement or necessity — all the power of the day in a few hours, and sometimes in one grand effort. Such an one will not, when interested in work, realize that he is becoming weary, but his task finished or his strength spent, he will find himself exhausted. This is the hand of the advanced thinker and worker.

Soft Hands belong to one who labors with fatigue and weariness, to whom heavy work or continued activity is a hardship. Continued activity at light service is, however, easier than the expenditure of strength. Its characteristics of work are like the elastic but less enthusiastic and less enduring and without the rapid recuperative power of the latter.

The Plastic Hand which is very soft and non-elastic, announces one lacking in physical strength and activity — void of endurance — a low state of muscular and vital forces. The plastic hand, warm — a very rare occurrence — will suggest a diseased brain, a weak mind, indolence and selfishness. Moderately warm will suggest a recent severe illness, with promise of restored health. Cold, it will show long continued ill-health with little prospect of immediate improvement. Cold and damp — or worse if moist — will indicate disease of the lungs, and, in some cases, secret vices undermining the vitality and destroying the health.

Resume. — The hard hands show strong enduring muscular power and continued activity. The elastic hand is vital rather than muscular; energetic rather than enduring; inclined to crowd its work into a short time, or mass the entire strength and vitality into sharp, rapid, effective effort. The soft hand has little muscular endurance, but is graceful, delicate and active in light work. It is impressionable and often accompanies clear, continuous mental effort. The plastic hand is weak, passive, and inert. Hard hands love travel and adventure. Soft hands love to hear of them. Hard hands may be strong in their attachments, self-denying and helpful, without much show of tenderness. Soft hands will exhibit more tenderness, more passive endurance, without being more faithful; more ardent without being more firm in their affection. Hard hands show little impressionability — appreciate exact and tangible realities. Soft hands are impressionable, and given to reverie and imagination, loving the marvelous and the mysterious. Hard hands have power, and use it for active resistance; soft hands excel in passive endurance. Hard hands with smooth and pointed fingers will suggest traders and trainers of horses and other animals, while soft hands of like form will tell of one who loves to engage in like pursuits theoretically — adventure in the library or on the stage.

Women with large palms, especially as they are elastic or soft, and particularly if the lines show good health and recuperative power, will bear children with comparative ease. On the contrary women with small palms, especially as they are firm or hard, and particularly if the lines show ill health or low vitality, will suffer much in child-bearing.

The Skin of the hand, fairly warm, evenly colored, delicate and clinging, indicates good health. The skin too white suggests a cold temperament, lack of strong attachments, selfishness and egotism; too red, shows heated blood, coarseness, violent anger, strong passions. Both extremes are very undesirable.

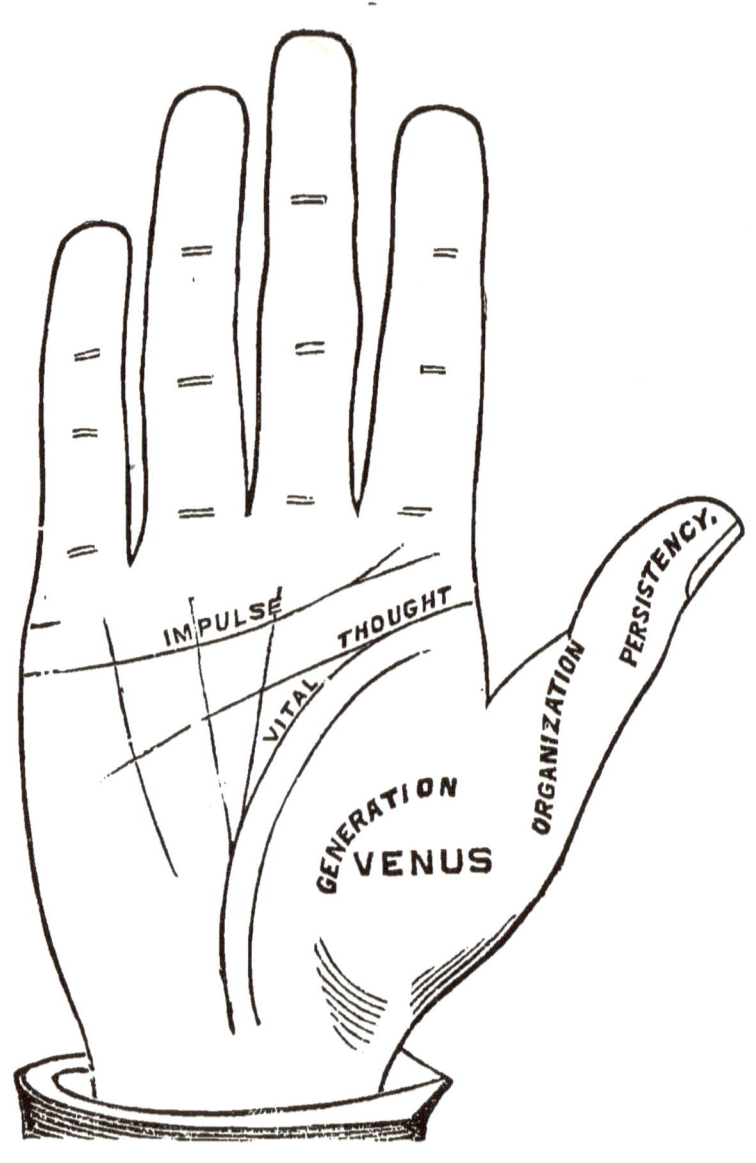

THE THUMB.

CHAPTER IV.

THE THUMB.

THE superior animal is found in the hand, humanity in the thumb, says a celebrated authority. "In default of other proofs," said Newton, "the thumb would convince me of the existence of God." Many expressions in literature and in the popular, as well as the provincial idioms, refer to the supposed power and influence of the thumb. Superstitious people cover the thumb to avoid the danger threatened by the "evil eye." In all occult matters the thumb plays a prominent part. Shakespeare frequently refers to the thumb. Biting the thumb, as noticed in Romeo and Juliet, is an old and forcible method of bestowing an intentional insult. The witches consulted their thumbs as prophetic, and are made to say

"By the pricking of my thumbs
Something wicked this way comes."

History and the Bible refer to the heathen and Israelitish practice of mutilating their prisoners of war by cutting off their thumbs. When the fallen and vanquished gladiator, in the Roman arena, saw the spectators with "thumbs up" his heart rejoiced, for he then knew that his bravery, though overcome, had won for him life and freedom. But when the thumbs pointed downward he shut his eyes, resigning hope, and closing his fingers over his thumb, awaited the ordered and speedily given death blow.

In idiots, who are guided by impulse only, the thumbs are small and often withered or deformed, and are usually concealed beneath the overclasping fingers. Infants and feeble-minded people, in closing the hand, double the fingers over the thumb. In both cases, however, as intelligence dawns, and as there is any exhibition of will or choice, the thumb asserts its supremacy by doubling over the fingers. When the premonitions of an epileptic fit come on, the thumb becomes inert, and during the spasm the thumb is usually hid in the palm under the fingers. When the great darkness of death settles about the glazing eye, the fingers shut over the thumb and bury it.

Upon the length and strength, proportion and mobility of the thumb depends largely the powers and adaptability of the hand.

The large fleshy ball formed by the muscles of the thumb in the lower part of the palm upon which its strength depends is the distinguishing characteristic of the human hand, and especially of the strong and expert hand.

The thumb acts as a controlling helper of the fingers, either singly or in any combination, and in a hand of average flexibility can touch any phalange of any finger. The thumb, too, at once controls and coöperates with the fingers, by acting in opposition to them. It thus beautifully symbolizes, what it also represents, the intellectual force, which clearly appreciates and wisely directs the other powers, which by firm control — sometimes by kind repression, often by friendly opposition — developing the mental peculiarities and affectional impulses and utilizing the animal powers.

The thumb indicates the intelligent will. In general, a large thumb shows decision of character, persistency of purpose, and, therefore one likely to succeed. A small thumb will, therefore, show one who is vacillating and uncertain in his aims, and intermittent as well as changeable in his efforts.

The First Phalange of the thumb represents the will — the power of decision, continuity of purpose, and executive force. Persons who have this phalange long and strong will have a powerful and energetic will, great continuity of purpose and an extreme desire, expressed in persistent effort, to carry out any project undertaken. They will be able to control their appetites, passions and impulses; to continue in a project undertaken even though it be disagreeable, wearisome, or discouraging. This phalange long and the second short will indicate one who is disposed

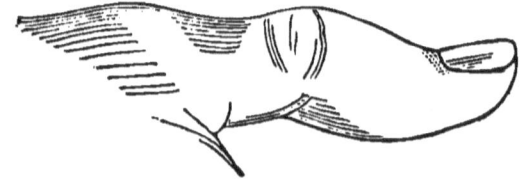

THE THUMB—First phalange long, second short.

towards domination, arbitrary rule and tyranny. If very large and rounding — ball-shaped — it attests extreme rashness and ungovernable fits of passion and combativeness. If the second phalange is weak it will show quarrelsomeness, petty cruelty, &c.

The first phalange medium represents passive resistance — inertia — and shows a person moderate in will, yet sometimes subject to outside pressure or to the force of emotion and appetite.

This phalange short shows lack of steadfast

resolution; indicates one who does not and cannot always control himself; one who is disposed to adopt the opinions and be controlled by the will of others.

This phalange short and broad indicates obstinacy and prejudice. The short phalange indicates indecision and unfixedness, and the breadth shows strength of will. Extreme in its joys and sorrows, and above all in its passions, this phalange is the index (the second phalange weak) of ungoverned and ever-changing whims and prejudice.

The first phalange very short and feeble shows powerlessness to resist, indifference to the duties of life — discouragements and enthusiasms by turn, sadness and gayety without adequate cause.

One with this phalange weak can never be implicitly relied upon for steadfastness even in friendship or love. Such an one may be devoted but not constant — honest and ardent, but not consistent and persistent.

The Second Phalange represents the intellect, judgment, plan. This phalange long and strong, shows that the intellect is clear and reliable; the power of planning and organizing is present in superior measure. This phalange short and weak, indexes little intellectual stamina, defective and sluggish judgment, dim and vacillating views, with changing purposes.

The first and second phalanges of equal length and strength and a thumb in full proportion to the balance of the hand, shows intelligent use of knowledge, powers of planning and organizing, with will and continuity of purpose to execute, and may well be denominated the "ideal thumb."

THE THUMB—Second phalange long, first short.

The second phalange long and strong and the first weak, indicates one with more judgment than will, more plan than execution. His ideas and purposes may be excellent, but a hesitancy to act prevents their execution. His perception may suggest the propriety of the plan while his judgment approves and points out the necessity of immediate and persistent advance; but he lacks the resolution to proceed. Caution, prudence and indecision become the apologies for vacillation and inaction. Such an one may be a good counsellor but a poor executive, a good subordinate but a poor leader.

The Third Phalange of the thumb — the "Mount of Venus" — will be fully described and interpreted under that heading. This phalange represents the physical man as to strength and vitality. Large, full and bounding, it attests great physical strength; firmness asserts corresponding endurance; a fair temperature and color shows large vitality; extreme hardness suggests strong and persistent animal appetites; if sinewy and elastic, it shows activity, vigor, impetuosity; softness indicates impressionability, delicacy and keenness of appetite and passion, and intensity of sensuous impulses; very soft — which rarely occurs with a full development — suggests as other characteristics determine, the indolent dilettante, the epicure, the gourmand, the voluptuary — the one dreaming of sensuous exercises which he is too indolent or too impotent to make sensuous realities. Most debauchees, voluptuaries, lecherous men and wanton and abandoned women have the root of the thumb full and the other phalanges, especially the first, short or feeble.

The third phalange feeble or flat marks little physical strength, low vitality, lack of endurance and a deficiency in sensuous appetite.

Resume. — The whole thumb more fully developed than in proportion with the hand, shows a tendency to domination; very large, indicates calculating tyranny. Under medium size it indicates passive resistance, and very small shows a person subject to his own passion or impulse, and to the direction and control of others.

The first phalange strong with the second weak, indicates one who is erratic, rash, impulsive, dominant, arbitrarily tyrannical, self-assertive, &c., as the other peculiarities determine. The second phalange strong, the first weak, will show one of good judgment, plan, and intelligence, but of little executive ability and of vacillating purpose, lacking continuity and persistance of application.

The purposes for which, and the directions in which, the qualities thus indicated are expended must be determined from the other peculiarities of the affections and thoughts.

He who has the third phalange of the thumb full — showing great physical power, elastic — showing strong sensuous impulse, the second also full and long, indicating intelligent plan and definite purpose, with the first likewise fully developed — telling of firm decision and persistent and continuous effort, must be a leader. He may develop into the daring general, leading armies; the successful manager of large concerns, molding the muscular powers of the many into material products, profitable to them and himself; the philanthropist, spending his strength for the race; the missionary or martyr, devoting his life enthusiastically to his faith; or he may be the calculating, persistent, successful enemy of virtue — the confirmed sensualist.

One thing may always be certified, the person with the three phalanges of the thumb full and strong, and equally developed, will be no ordinary individual. Such an one will always be forcible, intelligent and effective. Rarely, however, will such an one bear a character of unmixed good or evil. Such a thumb always belongs to one of marked power; and, usually, to one who, whatever his general character, has great physical strength, sensuous keenness, and dominating tendencies — great temptations, clear and decided plans, indomitable perseverance — and, hence, unusual success.

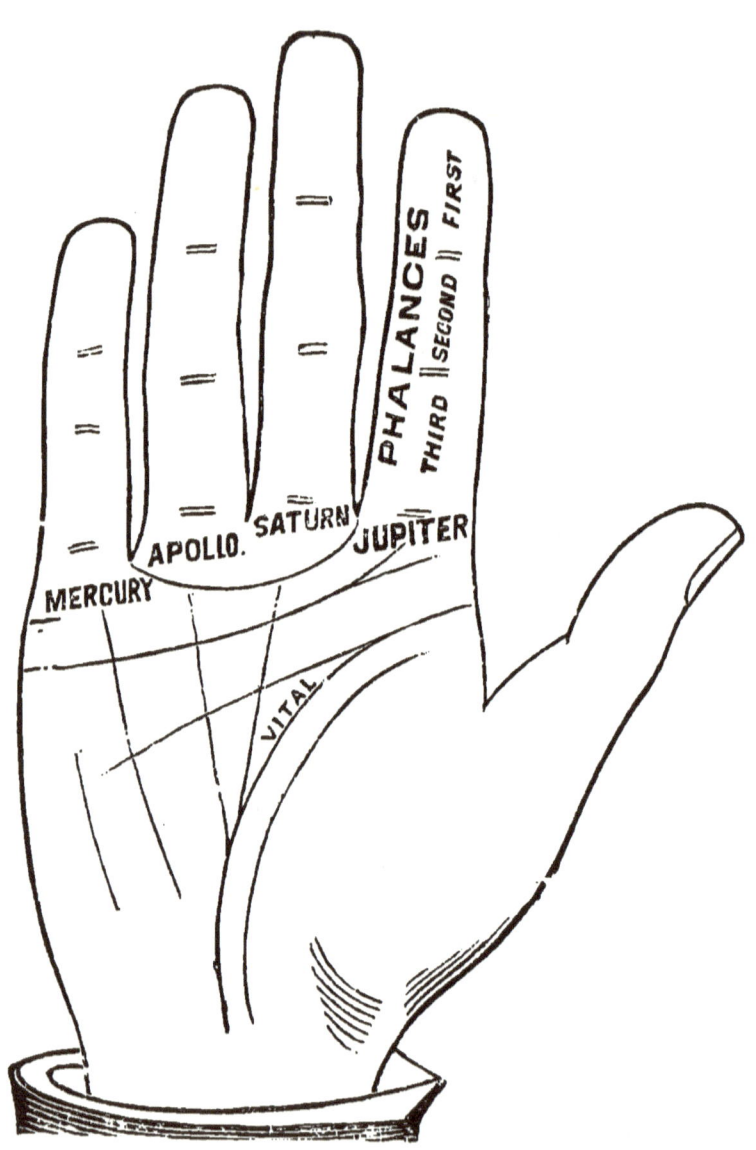

DIVISION OF THE FINGERS.

CHAPTER V.

THE FINGERS.

THE fingers have special features easily recognized. They may be anywhere between the extremes of long and short; smooth, undulating, or knotted at the joints; fleshy, and then firm, puffy or flabby — or lean, and then trim, skinny or shrunken; uniform in size or tapering; spatulate, square, oval or pointed at the ends; straight, curved or crooked; symmetrical or ill-shapen. Any one finger may be of almost any combination of the above peculiarities, and other fingers on the same hand of some other combinations. It will usually be found that one finger is more tapering and pointed than the others, another more knotted than its fellows, and one knot larger than the other, and that the corresponding fingers on the right and left hands are of different lengths, actually and in proportion to their fellows. These peculiarities are all to be noticed, as each one of them indicates some characteristic of the person.

The fingers index the tastes, direction of abilities, and manipulating peculiarities. The lower phalanges tell of the material and selfish tendencies; the middle, of the intellectual character; and the upper ones, or first phalanges, indicate the inspirational and manipulating abilities and show the direction naturally followed in the activities of life.

Short Fingers indicate one who sees in general, examines only the mass, recognizes the whole, comprehends the *tout ensemble*. Persons with short fingers see the whole effect, and comprehend it, before they notice or appreciate the parts; they love the large, the majestic, the sublime, but do not equally value the details. They work in general with a long, free, swinging stroke, and produce strong effects. Their work will usually be graceful — not exact or intricate. They value a person as a whole, before they know his detailed accomplishments. They admire friends for acceptable strong points, notwithstanding minor faults, which they either do not see; or seeing, ignore. They know many persons and their strong peculiarities, but notice few of their ordinary characteristics. They know if a person is good-looking or well-dressed, but often not the color of the hair or eyes, or the material or style of the dress.

All these peculiarities attested by short fingers are intensified if the fingers are smooth or tapering and the hand soft. Cruelty is suggested by very short, thick, stubbed fingers, especially with a hard hand and the lines full and red.

Long Fingers indicate a person who sees the parts, appreciates the details and understands the minutia, and from their consideration determines the whole. Such persons will prefer the exact to the colossal, thorough finish to greatness of plan, the elegant to the grand. As mechanics they excel in intricate work, nice adjustment and completeness of finish; as artists they are characterized — much like the large hands — by their excellence in minute work, and by the care bestowed upon exact finish; as orators or conversationists they will be characterized by the use of illustrations, digressions, particularity of statement, fullness of description, which in excess may obscure the argument or hide the main point in a multitude of unimportant trivialities.

Long, knotted and straggling fingers will suggest intrigue, chicanery, querulousnes, useless care on unimportant side-issues, unnecessary labor spent in unproductive minutia.

These characteristics are shown strengthened as the fingers are knotted and the palm is long and firm. The average middle finger is in length nearly equal to the palm.

There is no fixed, or even medium proportion for the lengths of the different fingers. The middle one is, almost without exception, the longest, and the little finger the shortest. The first finger is generally shorter than the third, often, however, equal to it, frequently longer, but very rarely as long as the middle one. The third finger is usually longer than the first, but seldom as long as the middle one.

The variation between the lengths of the fingers on the right and left hands, both actually and comparatively, may best be seen by comparing the first and third with each other, and with the middle finger; and the little one with the third finger.

Any finger as it is long intensifies the character of the mount at its base, which also is modified in turn by the peculiarity of the finger.

Smooth Fingers signify intuition, immediate perception, rapid comprehension of ideas and things presented. Persons with smooth fin-

KNOTTED FINGERS. 77

gers will at once incline to accept or reject the thought brought forward. They largely depend upon their perception — more easily see and understand than demonstrate or analyze. They appreciate and use clear statements, illustrations and examples, rather than arguments and deductions. They see human nature rather than judge it. They know people by perception rather than estimate them by calculation. Their first impressions are usually not only clear but also true.

Smooth fingers, if pointed, have little order; if square, they love the sight and idea of order; if spatulated they will have moderate order — if time allow. Smooth and transparent fingers suggest curiosity — if pointed, levity. All the indications of the smooth fingers are strengthened as they are also tapering; and intensified as the hand is soft and the skin delicate, showing also impressionability — suggesting also the artist and poet.

Knotted Fingers indicate order, logic, deduction — and in excess, with other characteristics concurring, — skepticism, distrust, suspicion, etc. Persons with knotted fingers want the logic of truths and facts — the motive for doing — the why and wherefore of belief.

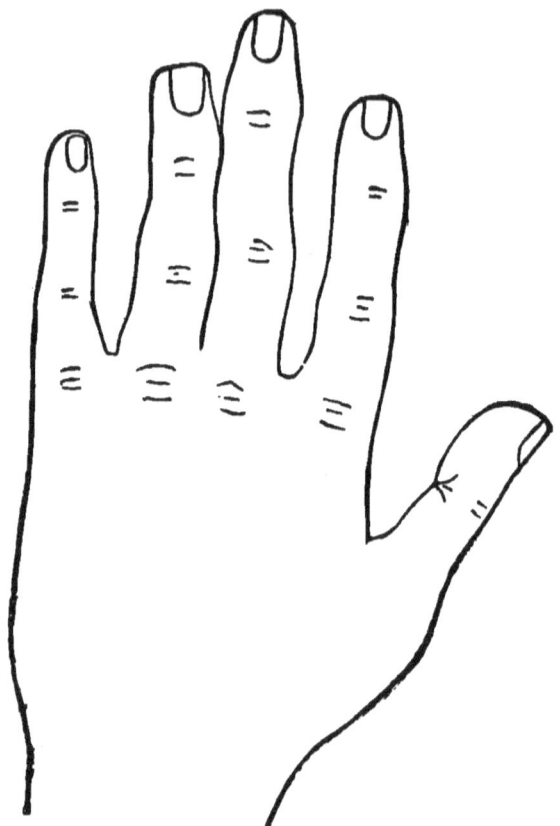

KNOTTED FINGERS—Square and Oval.

The Logical Knot, below the first phalange, attests order in intellectual work, arrangement of ideas, classification of moral and mental causes and results, method in philosophical and religious researches and deductions. Persons with this knot doubt, reason, deduce, conclude. They may value evidence, but want arguments. They may desire testimony, but they require demonstration. Without ignoring experience they exalt logic.

In excess, or in a weak hand, this knot is the index of a mind prone to indulge in petty distinctions, unrest, fault-finding, hair-splitting, captious and useless deductions. Persons with this knot and a long, pointed first phalange, will struggle between ideality and logic, and may have by turns (other qualities concurring) the ecstasies of the poet and the doubts of the philosopher — the assurances of the fanatic and the disbelief of the skeptic. They will often feel or see one set of truths from inspiration or intuition, while logically they deduce and hence believe another, and perhaps a contradictory doctrine, and will act as one or the other rules the moment, thus exhibiting erratic ideas and actions.

Persons with this knot and square finger-ends will see clearly, justly, practically, and test the impressions and perceptions by logic; requiring that poesy, art, religion and philosophy be reasonable and practical. They will be more pious than devout; more moral than ceremonial. They may love the beautiful, but will be apt to identify it with the true and especially with the useful — which they will place parallel with the good. They will value law, defer to usage, and quote precedent and justice. They will be effective in realizing their conceptions, practical in their plans and work, and careful, exact, and faithful in their manipulations.

This knot with spatulated fingers shows one who calculates how his ideas may be turned into action, calculates speed, movement, change. Such persons love independence, rely upon themselves, value their own opinions rather than precedent, and, with a large thumb, force their will and way.

The Knot of Material Order — below the second phalange — shows calculation, deduction, reason, order, connected with material and tangible interests — the logic of ideas connected with matter. Persons with this knot are inclined to investigate the method of a fact as well as its occurrence. In chemistry they see the experiment, but also want to know the law governing it. They accept the facts of sense if they appear reasonable; and accept the laws of reason if they are profitable. This knot belongs to the engineer, architect, business man, manufacturer, accountant, etc. In excess, and in otherwise weak hands this knot will suggest indecision, fussiness, petty carefulness, "too many irons in the fire."

TAPERING FINGERS. 81

The characteristics indicated by the knotted fingers are strengthened as the fingers are long, and intensified as the hand is firm or hard. Their value also depends upon whether the logical knot or the knot of material order predominates over the other. Their particular meaning also depends upon the interpretation of the finger showing the fuller development.

Tapering Fingers.—Slightly tapering fingers are guided more by plan and the ideal, and as the taper increases, the hand and the whole life is more and more subordinated to ideality. When the taper is decided and regular the ideal is shown and also the desire to see plan or ideal in sensuous form; and when such a hand carries also a graceful square-ended finger it attests the superior ability to sensuously express the imagined forms, and, therefore, suggests the musician, painter, sculptor — poet. Small or medium, full, soft hands, with tapering, smooth and pointed or oval fingers, may give the world new ideas. The same hand with square finger-ends will value and describe the experiences. The larger hand with longer fingers and square ends, will, (especially if the palm is elastic), explain them. The "philosophic" hand, described hereafter, will logically deduce the naturally outflowing duty, action or benefit.

All peoples give their ideals tapering fingers. They are universal emblems of purity, poetry and perfection.

Large, Ungainly Fingers, of the same size at the ends as at the roots index one who is an unthinking plodder and drudge — the laborer who must be cared for and directed at each step by an overseer — one who puts no calculation, and very little care into his efforts.

Fingers lying close together so that no light is seen between them, especially if the fingers are irregular, suggest avarice, secrecy, and general selfishness.

THE FINGER-ENDS.

These 'eyes of the hand' may be spatulate, square, oval or pointed. Most hands present combinations or modifications of two or more of these varieties. In fact it frequently happens that a single hand, or pair of hands, will illustrate the four classes, thus forcibly exhibiting — not "the law of the members warring against the law of the mind," — but rather, different impulses, inclinations and ideals combating, interfering with, and thus modifying, each other.

The Spatulate form indicates physical activity, manual occupation, love of muscular exercise, locomotion. It suggests industrial pursuits and mechanics, constancy in the pur-

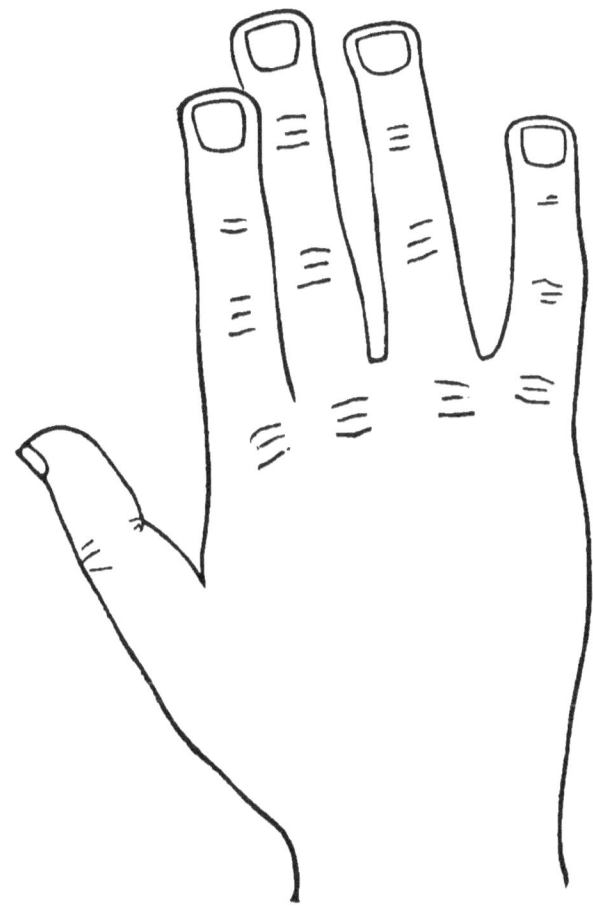

SPATULATE FINGERS – Slightly Undulating.

suit of material advantages and material comforts; adventure, riches, &c. It shows resolution rather than resignation. It prefers abundance to elegance, practical facts to poetic theories, the evils of labor rather than those of nature; active effort in overcoming hardship, rather than indolent luxury. The spatulate hand founds new colonies, builds up large productive industries, prefers the beauties of nature to those of art, and is inclined to sink the artist in the artizan. It delights in abundance and comfort; and while, unlike the elementary hand, considering them the only necessity, still estimates them above refinement and elegance. The love of the spatulate hand is ardent rather than tender, self-sacrificing rather than expressive, inclined to accept the good seen in the loved one rather than idealize the beloved. Its manners are hearty and hospitable rather than formal or polished.

Hands excessively spatulate suggest petulance.

Spatulate fingers on a hard or firm hand belong to one who rises with the sun, hunts, rows, swims, works ploddingly, continuously, and engages in contests of strength and endurance; in a word, he likes activity which also calls for the expenditure of muscular power. On an elastic hand they show one who works with enthusiasm, one who is expert and skillful, proud of his ability as a marksman, his superiority as a gymnast, his excellence as a workman; in short, one who will weave together his muscular strength, nervous activity and mental calculation. Spatulate fingers on a soft hand shows one who delights in seeing feats of strength and skill put forth by others. One who loves boating — if another rows. He will like expeditions and adventures — if he have horses or other transportation, and servants to do the drudgery of the campaign. He will excel in work where skill and moderate exertion is required. The hand very soft and spatulate will often suggest the epicure.

The Square Ended Fingers attest a mind and hand working cheerfully and harmoniously together. Persons with such fingers naturally want employment in which brain and hand, thought and action are together embodied in the result of their labor. Whether poet, philosopher or mechanic; artist, artizan or laborer; legislator, judge or executive; merchant, manufacturer or producer; the person with square finger ends will always clothe his inspirations, perceptions and calculations in clear expression and precise form, aiming to secure effective and definite results. The brain will constantly direct the hand, and the hand will be the efficient agent of the brain.

The great musical composers had square-ended fingers, moderately tapering, with knotted joints. Michael Angelo had similar fingers, only more tapering and both knots

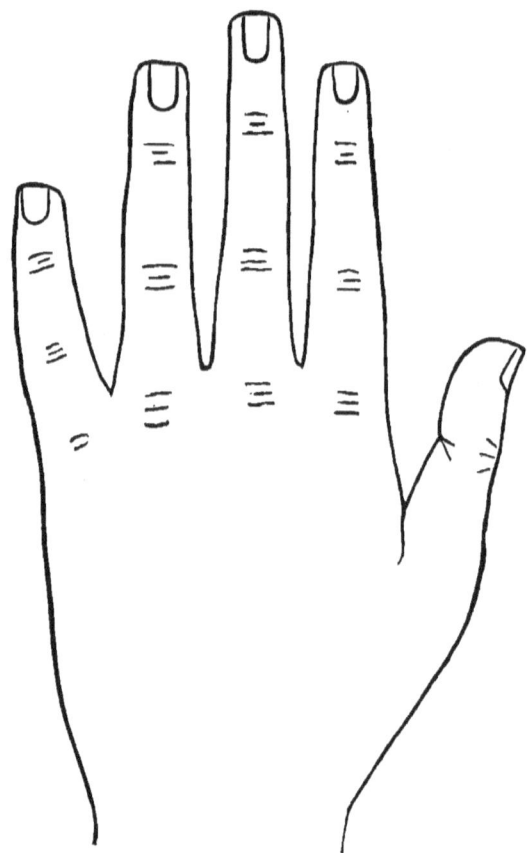

SQUARE FINGERS—Smooth and Tapering.

moderately large, and an immense thumb; accuracy, symmetry, detail, completeness, truthfulness, persistency and strength are his characteristics. Raphael had smooth, very tapering, square ended fingers and a moderate thumb; grace, purity of color, general warmth, moderate detail, lack of faithfulness in drawing, and an unequalled appeal to the perceptions and feelings belong to his works. Famous instrumental musicians, celebrated marksmen, skillful gymnasts, artizans and billiardists — in a word, those who are noted for the precision, finish and superiority of their manipulation — are characterized by square finger ends.

It must not be inferred that all square finger ends carry with them this celebrity. Square finger ends, however, attest superior power of manipulation, a love of practical and useful results, a keen sense of symmetry, rythm, truth and justice; a willingness to labor not for its own sake, nor simply for the pecuniary reward of labor, but rather for the immediate result of a superior product, with more satisfaction in the success of good work than in the pay for the exertion put forth. The excess, or rather, the ill use of this power, is useless care and unnecessary exactness and finish when not needed, which does not belong to the finger ends, but to the large knots, or perverse Jupiter.

The Oval finger-ends attest ideality, contemplation, grace of posture and movement.

88 THE FINGERS.

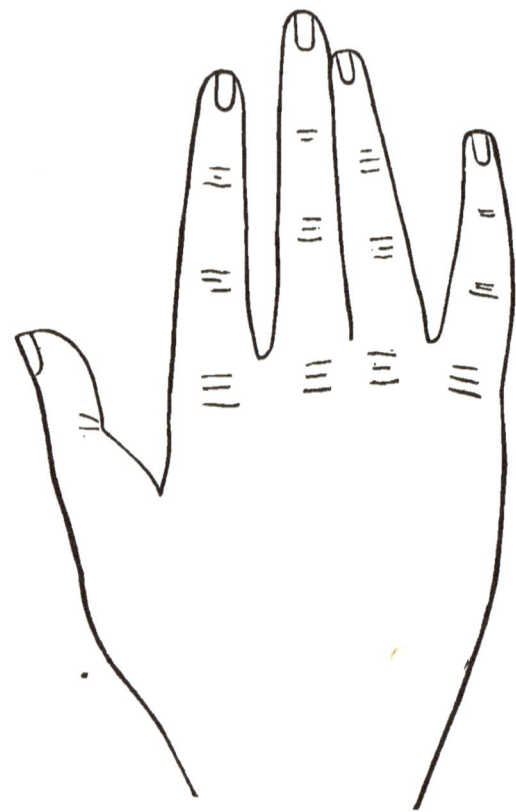

OVAL FINGERS—Tapering and Smooth.

The artistic taste and the poetic sentiment here rule the life. A love of sculpture, painting, song, poetry, is suggested. The æsthetic taste is present, with ability to appreciate, understand and criticize, without however, superior power to create. Grace is valued, rather than truth, form rather than strength, ornament rather than use, suggestion rather than fulness, delicacy rather than exactness. Imagination and ideality rule the hand and its manipulations, the life and its activities, and we hear the murmur:

"Come let us worship beauty."

Other characteristics concurring, the oval finger-end will suggest religion, divination, ecstasy. In a weak hand it will hint at falling from artistic flights after the imagined perfection into dreamy and indefinite reverie, and may show one who is erratic, unreliable and impure, who will, however, in degradation even, always exhibit fancy, grace and romance.

The Pointed finger-ends attest a person fanciful, erratic, romantic, impractical, changeable, sometimes unreliable — always peculiar. Persons with pointed fingers are characterized by movements quick and graceful, but not usually exact or effective. They are apt to mistake a part, clearly seen, for the whole; a single instance* for a general truth.

---

* The person, who in New York saw an Arkansas trader in leather breeches, coon-skin cap and navy revolver, and who wrote "home" to England, that the people of the Mississippi Valley were a peculiar race who dressed in buckskin clothes, coon-skin caps and navy five-shooters, was probably endowed with short, smooth, pointed fingers.

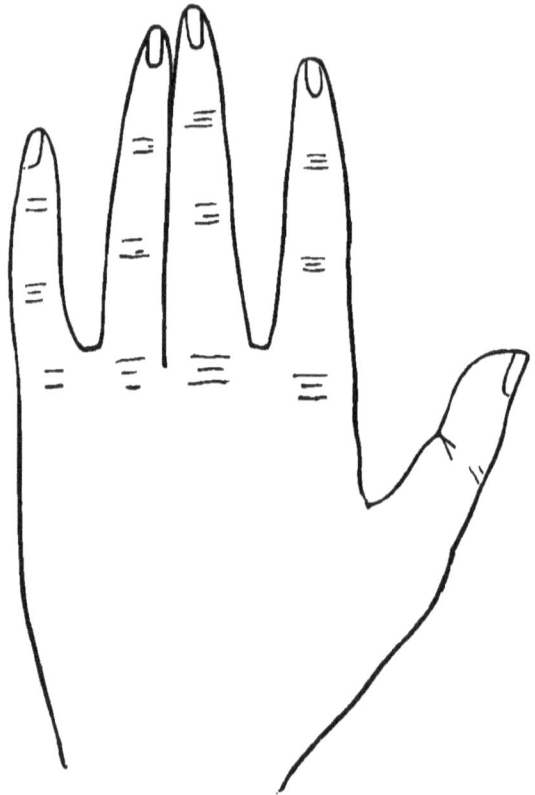

POINTED FINGERS—Very Tapering.

They may be brilliant in some directions, but not generally even or constant. The flashing fancy, the brilliant sally, the burst of enthusiasm, the wail of despair, exaggerated danger, or magnified joy, are all suggested according as other signs concur. Pointed fingers may indicate an irregular and unsym-

THE PHALANGES. 91

metrical genius — one eminent for a few peculiar and noticeable excellencies, accompanied by just as noticeable defects — one who lacks the "definite proportion of faculty."

The pointed fingers must not be confounded with the tapering ones. They are often found supplementing and intensifying each other, but their meanings are distinct.

The fingers on any pair of hands are usually various in character as to knots and the shape of the ends. The first finger is usually the more pointed, and the middle one the more spatulate. The third finger is characterized by the square form, and the little one is often oval.

THE PHALANGES are compared with each other to determine which characteristic will rule the others, and thus find the practical development.

The First Phalange, carrying the nail, as it is long indexes originality, imagination, invention, inspiration, fantasy. Short, the lack of these endowments.

The Second Phalange long and full shows perception, thought, reason — activity of brain. Short, the contrary.

The Third Phalange — next to the palm — long, attests material tendencies, and large or full shows selfishness, avarice, etc. Short, the contrary. The third phalange lean, indicates impulsive liberality.

THE FIRST FINGER indexes the qualities as noted under the Mount of Apollo. As it is long these qualities are shown intensified. As it is short they are weak. Grills on this finger suggest a merry person. Perpendicular lines suggest industry, love of manipulation.

The first phalange long shows inspiration and originality in art, religion and ambition; short, lack of these. Pointed shows a tendency to contemplation, spiritism, and, other signs concurring, to mysticism, fanaticism, vanity, etc. Square, shows the love of truth for its own sake, ideality directed to social relations, the practical in art, and the actual in religion, with ambition strong and attainable. Spatulate, which is rare, suggests restless speculation, activity in ideal experiments, —exaggerated mysticism, superstition.

The second phalange suggests intelligence, plans, and ambition intense as the part is long; strong as it is full.

The third phalange will tell of the actual effort put forth to attain the ideal shown in the first phalange, and planned in the second. Too full and long will suggest vanity, selfishness, desire for prominence, etc. Perpendic-

THE SECOND FINGER. 93

ular lines in this phalange suggest purity, warm-heartedness, etc.

THE SECOND FINGER is interpreted by and also supplements and modifies the meaning of the Mount of Saturn at its base. Very long it shows earnestness, carefulness, sadness, fatality.

The first phalange as it is long shows original ideas of the value, use, and happiness of life; very long suggests sadness, depressed spirits, imaginary evils. Pointed, which is rare, shows inordinate selfishness, frivolity and folly. Square — a mind directed to the effective, practical, useful, honorable in dealing. Spatulate shows one who values the material aspect of life. With other signs concurring, we have suggested struggles, despondency, sad forebodings, painful memories.

The second phalange as it is long shows love of science, exact and practical when the fingers are knotted — the occult and speculative when the fingers are smooth. Also love of history and love of exact plan.

The third phalange marks interest in material things and personal care. Full and long it shows thrift, economy, riches, avarice, selfish grasping as other tendencies determine. A star or grill here suggests an overbearing and tyrannical person—one brooking no opposition.

THE THIRD FINGER long shows one who is devoted to truth, art, riches, glory.

The first phalange as it is long shows invention and originality in the above matters. Very pointed suggests one who is an idealist, and moderately pointed one who rides some special hobby, or else dabbles in many lines of expression — as the thumb is strong or weak — who may be brilliant, not exact; eccentric and uneven in his work. It will in some hands suggest criticism, boasting, prejudice. Square shows a love of defined art, truthfulness of expression, fulness of rendition, ability to realize in good form the person's ideals. Spatulate will suggest one who appreciates the poetry of motion, love of high colors, battle-scenes, etc. Also ability and love of organizing military displays. One who loves exhibitions of strength and skill, speed and endurance, and who enjoys the "business" in a dramatic representation.

The second phalange long exhibits the reasoning in art, truthfulness of conception and execution, and the effort to classify and harmonize the ideas.

The third phalange long will suggest the material bias in artistic work, the pursuit of art for its profits, the builder of machinery, the duplication of popular works — the artist who thinks more of his gains and glory than of his embodied ideals, more of his reputation than of his ability.

THE LITTLE FINGER indexes abstract science and numbers. As it is long it shows a love of expression and of explaining and imparting instruction; ability and readiness to assert, demonstrate and maintain one's ideas, plans and position. Thus in a strong hand, ability as a speaker; in a moderate hand, readiness as a counsellor, friend and helper; in a weak hand it will suggest the egotist, the boaster, the intrusive one, the tyrant. Illy formed perpendicular lines on the outer edge of this finger, especially if they run through all the phalanges, suggest hypocrisy, deception, dishonesty, theft, robbery, as other signs may interpret.

Bashful and reticent people exhibit the little finger falling short of the first knot of the third finger.

The first phalange long suggests the theorist who loves new laws and theories, which are invented or mastered for their own sake — the student. Pointed, is an inclination to mysticism — often the brilliant conversationist. Square, a love of science applied; facility in conveying ideas; by clear and full statement and illustration. If the finger is undulating or knotty and the second phalange long, the presentation will be exact, careful and logical. Spatulate, suggests scientific movement, bodily activity, gesture and emphasis in oratory, ability in operating machinery, slight of hand, jugglery, &c. With bad accompanying characteristics the spatulate phalange will here suggest theft. The second phalange favorable indicates intelligent industry, power of organization, management of business; and with an otherwise bad hand, the confidence operator and trickster. The third phalange long shows, as other characteristics may indicate, the use of science for material results; the acquisition of property, reputation, advantage; subtlety, avarice, intrigue, dishonesty, theft. Short and weak, the third phalange will indicate little power of material or selfish accumulation.

Round Fingers, that is, fingers, cross sections of which, especially of the first phalanges, are circular, suggest a person who is reticent, and a diffidence or unwillingness to boldly express the thoughts or plans.

Elliptical Fingers, thinner from the nail to the inside of the phalange than transversely, especially as they become flat, show openness, frankness and ease of statement.

REVIEW.

Short Fingers appreciate and love magnitude, grace, generalities; they see the mass, judge of the whole, and afterwards perceive, examine or appreciate the parts or particulars.

Long Fingers, on the contrary, are characterized by minutia, elegance, finish; they perceive the details, understand the parts individually, and from them appreciate or estimate the mass or general effect.

Smooth Fingers signify perception, intuition and rapid determination. They want clear statement, illustration, testimony and metaphor.

Knotted Fingers tell of logic, argument, the why and wherefore, the thus and therefore. They demand premises, syllogisms and deductions. The first knot suggests order in ideas; the second, order in material things.

Tapering Fingers show the rule of the ideal, and love of that ideal sensuously expressed.

Stubbed Fingers, the same size at ends as at the palms, will indicate in good hands the superior manipulator; in poor hands the plodder.

THE NAILS.

The nails will repay careful study, for experience only will enable the reader to fully appreciate the delicate shades of difference between the permanent and transitory variations in their color and general appearance.

Long Nails indicate a peacemaker, one who will bear much for the sake of quiet; who is steadfast in friendship. Long nails are one of the indications of the diplomatist; also of the person who is suspicious.

Short Nails signal one who will assert and maintain his rights, and insist upon the honor or deference his due, and hence when perverted shows a jealous and contentious person. With the skin high upon  them they suggest pugnacity, or with a large thumb malevolence, criticism, mockery, contradiction, quizzing.

Broad Nails announce gentleness of disposition, a spirit of submission, bashfulness, and hence, sometimes, mean cowardice.

Narrow Nails show activity, a love of excitement and of directing others. They indicate a love of field sports and of practical joking. The evil signs are of a mischievous disposition, petty tyranny — cruelty.

Round Nails announce an honest disposition, a quick temper and if thin and delicate rapid reconciliation. Small round nails suggest obstinate anger, a tendency to hatred.

Fan-Shaped Nails announce envy and vanity.

Oblique Nails show deceitfulness and cunning cowardice. Large turned-in nails suggest dishonest ambition.

Small turned-in nails suggest vanity and forcible intent to achieve success.

Crooked and irregular nails signify petty cruelty.

Nails curved transversely show kindness and sympathy; curved lengthwise suggest rapacity.

Pink nails show a healthy, active, sanguine person. Thin, pink, elastic nails show sensitiveness, delicate organization. Extreme thinness will suggest one irritable and notional.

Red nails show an ardent temperament, an active brain and sometimes brain disease.

Bluish or purple nails announce disease of the liver or kidneys.

White nails show a phlegmatic temperament; very white, they indicate sickness and an inclination or liability to low type of fever, especially if they are also long.

Large white half-moons at the base of the nails announce a frank, open-hearted person who naturally speaks his thoughts and tells his plans and purposes; one who naturally tells what he sees or thinks, and repeats what he hears or learns. He may keep a secret, but it requires an effort. As this disposition decreases these "half-moons" lessen, until the naturally secretive person—who is "close as an oyster," has no vestige of them left.

Pale spots on the nails, especially near the base, indicate disease of the nerves, and an inclination to melancholy.

Red spots or blotches show a nervous irritation, that manifests itself in a choleric temper and a quarrelsome demeanor.

Horny nails suggest little delicacy.

Spongy nails usually show one not given to labor; a lover of ease, selfish and envious.

Pale and dark mixed nails show disease— with deceitful tendencies.

Swarthy nails suggest parsimony — a miser.

CHAPTER VI.

THE MOUNTS OF THE HAND.

THE palm of the hand was, by the ancient chiromantists, laid off into different localities, and these localities were named in honor of their principal deities. This division of the hand and the naming of the mounts was not an accidental or arbitrary matter, but was founded upon, and was the result of, careful and extended observation. They believed that their deities, each one of whom was credited with peculiar and well defined characteristics, were real and powerful personages. They believed that each one of these deities impressed upon or communicated to sublunary mortals his or her peculiar ability or disposition by association or contact with those mortals. These chiromantists also believed that this association and contact was most close, intimate and effective in controlling and moulding the character through the mediumship and instrumentality of the hand. They noticed that the hands of different persons were differently developed. Observation disclosed to them that the character attributed to Jupiter was most conspicuous in those persons having a full and clear mount at the base of a long and gracefully formed first finger. This locality was therefore dedicated to that god, and named the "Mount of Jupiter." In like manner they discovered which peculiarities of character and which development of mounts were associated together in the same person's life and hand, and named the other mounts accordingly. The names thus assigned have ever since been adopted and retained by those who have studied or practiced chiromancy, either for character reading, or for so-called divination.

While utterly repudiating the theory of influence upon mortals by these gods and goddesses: and of course repudiating, as before stated, the later astrological theory of planetary influence, still the names of the different mounts and localities of the hand then bestowed will be adopted and used in this treatise.

THE MOUNTS IN GENERAL.—When interpreting a mount notice first its location — whether it is in exact position, and if not then towards what other mount or locality it is drawn. Next inquire whether it is full, moderate or depressed, and whether it is regular — full in the centre, or uneven — one part fuller than another. Then its color, and whether even or variegated. Notice also the lines — principal, secondary or accidental — which point towards, touch, cut or occupy the mount. The locality of the mount bears the name, whether elevated or depressed.

Mounts are favorable when they are (1) in proper position; (2) of fair size; (3) generous height; (4) well rounded on the centre; (5) of good even color; (6) smooth; (7) impressed with the appropriate principal lines; (8) or beautified with advantageous accidental lines or signs.

These eight elements are each a factor in the ideally perfect mount. Their modifications may be to give an excess, (except in position,) to lessen the perfection through all the shades of decrease, until they are entirely negative, and thus proceed to the opposite extremes.

A mount out of place is modified, sometimes controlled, by the mount towards which it tends; and this is good or ill as the controlling mount is favorable or not, and as it is better or worse than the mount drawn.

We cannot read the effect of any line or mount, or of any of its diverse modifications independently of the balance of the hand, but must carefully note all the powers and influences, and their mutual coöperations and antagonisms, and then deliberately and thoroughly calculate their combined results.

THE MOUNT OF VENUS occupies the base of the thumb, bounded by the vital line. This mount, in connection with the vital line, shows the physical man, his strength, intensity, endurance, elasticity, rapidity and kind of movement.

Venus favorable shows strong and enduring physical powers, intensity of action and animal impulse, sensuous appreciation and inclinations. The fullness is more especially indicative of the muscular development and strength in man, and of fullness of figure and beauty of form in woman; the fine quality of the mount points out grace in movement, beauty of action, melody in music, desire to please and be admired, ardent attachment, gallantry, elegance, love of sensuous pleasure, refined manners, or ideal and fanciful dissipation, as the other characteristics may determine. Its firmness or elasticity shows the enduring qualities of the person. A favorable color is the announcement of pure

MOUNTS OF THE HAND. 105

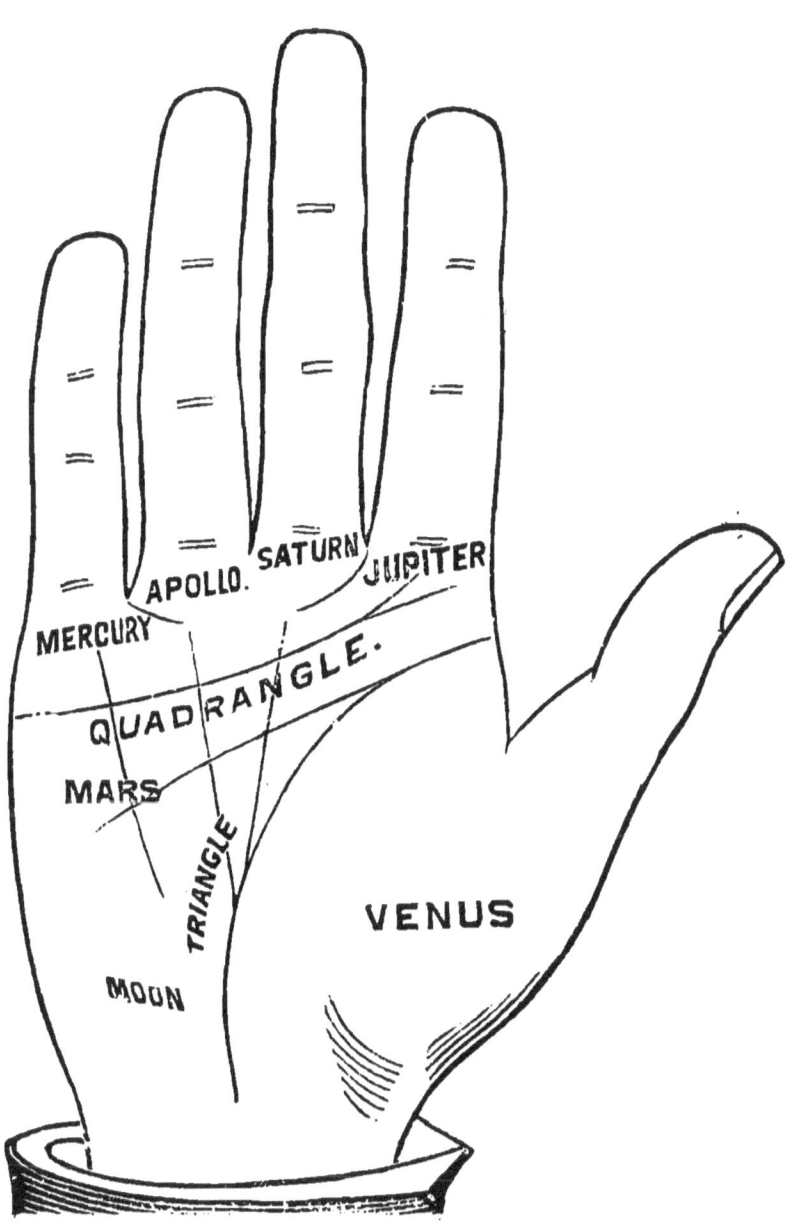

blood, good health, vitality and energy. Fullness here is desirable, while flatness or depression points out a weak physique, cold temperament, low vitality, poor health — a useless life. Whether the full mount of Venus shows a character of sensuality or philanthropy: of affection or selfish indulgence: of charity and tenderness or self-care and epicurianism: of debauchery or studious industry, depends upon the other characteristics of the person. This fullness points out the power, the endurance, the action, the grace of motion, the physical attractiveness of the person. The use — whether good or bad — made of this capital must be determined by consulting the other tendencies and abilities, shown in other parts of the hand. This mount full at the base and much lighter towards the supreme angle will show the sexual impulses strong as compared with the benevolent emotions, while the mount very full as it rises toward the natural line is to be expected in the philanthropist.

All lines on this mount parallel with the vital line are indicative of strength and endurance and of a legitimate and healthy use of the strength. Lines running across this mount, cutting these sister vital lines at right angles are of two kinds. The first are sharper in outline and higher in color, and are indications of intensity, excitement or irritation, and suggest excess or impurity as they are numerous, highly colored or strong, especially near the wrist. The second are finer, less deep and of a paler color and tell of depletion from illness — generally located in the lungs or nerve system. This difference easily seen in extreme cases, is sometimes so subtle as to baffle even the experienced eye. These cross-lines always point out irritation, unevenness of vitality, depletion, loss of power and endurance; but whether the person is to be pitied for his impurities or sympathized with for his misfortunes, can only be determined by determining first the cause of this loss of vitality and recuperating power. In doubtful cases — and they are many — charity will say sympathy, while candor and judgment will often say, mingled sympathy and pity.

Well-formed moderate sized lines on the mount of Venus, diagonally as to the vital line, point out an ardent and passionate person likely to be a favorite with voluptuous women. (See "*Accidental Lines,*" and page 69.)

THE MOUNT OF JUPITER is found in the upper part of the palm, between the impulse line and the root of the index finger — the finger that points, directs, orders, menaces, demonstrates and aspires.

Jupiter favorable indicates ideality, sensitiveness, refinement, enthusiasm. It may, therefore, point out ambition, pride, self-respect, love of art, honor, strong love attachments, sentimentality, religious fervor, æsthetic tastes, extremes of happiness or misery, immediate and intense likes and dislikes founded upon impressionability. A fair mount of Jupiter adds intensity to the intuitional and inspirational character and modifies the rational, skeptical and suspicious tendencies, lighting and warming them with imagination and affection.

When Jupiter is excessive it signifies the undue development of ideality and enthusiasm and may point out — as other parts of the hand may exhibit the accompanying characteristics of the person — vanity, egotism, arrogance, fanaticism or tyranny. With different associated peculiarities the prominent Jupiter may show fanciful but indefinite dilettanteism, mysticism, weak diffidence, visionary plans, many but unsettled purposes and often extremes of spiritual exaltation or depression. Jupiter weak or depressed indicates a mind lacking in or devoid of imagination and affection. It is thus found in the

MOUNT OF SATURN. 109

routine worker who is exact but without versatility; in him who needs a joke explained; in him who is just but hard; in the hand of one unjust and cruel; in him who may be affected through reason or evidence but without emotions. Jupiter full and smooth shows a happy disposition, ideal, aspiring, warm and calm. (See "*Accidental Lines*.)

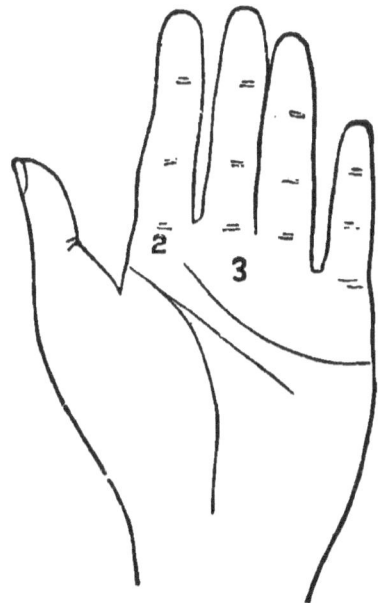

Mounts—Jupiter, [2.] Saturn, [3.]

THE MOUNT OF SATURN is found in the upper part of the palm under the root of the middle finger. Saturn indicates realism, seriousness and intensity of purpose. Saturn favorable shows ability, industry, prudence and energy in carrying out a determination. The person who has this mount favorable will succeed through the above qualities. This mount full, smooth and clear shows tranquillity, industry, hopeful views of life. One straight, clear, vertical line on this mount shows a determined, happy temperament. Several lines, especially if they are crooked or if they cut each other, will tell of irritation, cowardice, melancholy. Transverse lines attest fretfulness, perversity, melancholia, hypocondria.

In excess this mount will show a person who will go to extremes in accomplishing results; one who is taciturn or sad. He may love solitude, fear for future results, run into religious bigotry, cultivate asceticism, be inclined to suicide. Hence it will indicate extremes of views and efforts, which will often naturally lead to extremes of success or defeat.

This mount depressed or absent is just the opposite of the excessive and indicates an easy-going, care-nothing disposition, showing one who will fail to finish his undertaking — in fact a weak, often a useless, life.

Any transverse line in the hand, terminating under Saturn, is unfavorable. (See "*Accidental Lines.*")

MOUNT OF APOLLO.

THE MOUNT OF APOLLO, also called the Mount of the Sun, is in the upper part of the palm, under the base of the third finger. Apollo is beautiful, noble, charming, the god of the arts, and the patron of the artists.

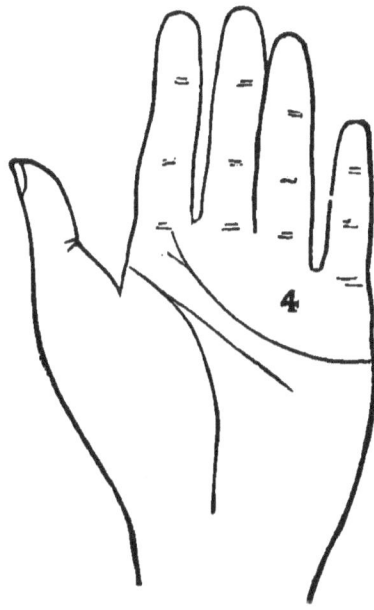

MOUNTS—Apollo, [4]

Apollo favorable indicates taste and ability in the arts, sculpture, music and poetry. It suggests ability to formulate and express the ideality, or to achieve the ambition shown by Jupiter. It suggests the ability and disposition to put in sensuous form the fancies and feelings, and to practically apply inventions: and hence hints at fame, honor amd satisfaction through artistic or literary success, or at riches through applied science. It also points out a hopeful and affectionate disposition, serenity of mind, warmth of heart, sympathy with humanity, and a religion affectionate, æsthetic and tolerant, rather than one of law and logic. It suggests hope and serenity of soul. In excess it shows vanity, vainglory, love of riches and celebrity, love of flattery; degenerating, other characteristics aiding, into boasting, levity, fanaticism, envy, dishonor and disgrace.

Absent or depressed shows lack of care or love for art, insensible to the power of beauty, without power to imagine or execute — a sunless day.

Vertical lines, clear and good, rising at the impulse line and passing up through Apollo, denote ability in practical application of art; powers of diplomacy and of gaining wealth. (See "*Accidental Lines*.")

THE MOUNT OF MERCURY is in the upper part of the palm, under the root of the little finger. Mercury favorable indicates a love of clear, exact, full knowledge — hence science; persuasive eloquence; personal influence through clearness of statement; gracious manners, promptitude of action, earnestness and enthusiasm. It shows ability,

MOUNT OF MERCURY. 113

and success based upon prompt, clear, persuasive presentation of the matter in hand; and hence is found in the hand of successful teachers, popular preachers, favorite society men, merchants, speculators, sharp debaters, and generally with those who talk better than they write, who charm by personal presence.

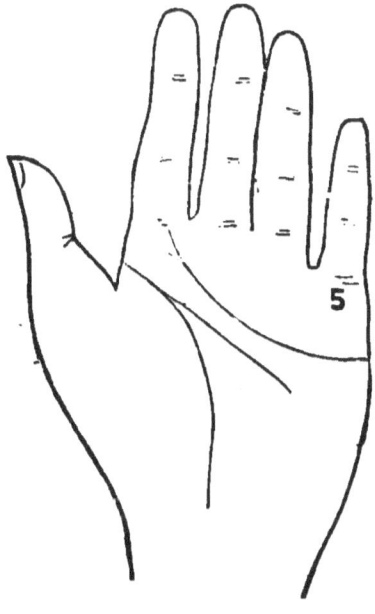

Mounts—Mercury, [5]

In excess it suggests deception, pretentious arrogance, dishonesty, theft, cheating and swindling — especially if cut by bad lines.

The mount absent or depressed will show one who speaks with diffidence, with little command of language, awkward manners and inapt for any business where he must come in contact with people. (See "*Accidental Lines.*")

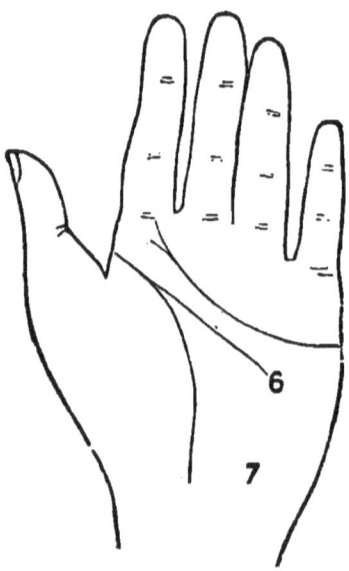

Mounts—Mars, [6] Moon, [7]

THE MOUNT OF MARS is found in the outer part of the palm between the impulse line and the Mount of the Moon. It extends from the percussion of the hand and loses itself in the Plain of Mars or hollow of the hand.

The Mount of Mars and the Plain of Mars favorable indicate courage, coolness and fearlessness in danger, self-reliance, strength, impetuosity and resignation. The mount shows these qualities active and aggressive; the plain indicates them passive, enduring and resisting. This mount and plain will bear a full development before there is an excess.

Mars excessive will suggest fool-hardiness, cruelty, violence, boorishness, tyranny and the like, while its depression or absence will mean non-resistance, cowardice, fear of danger, superstition and terror in accident.

The "fatal lines," which when found, are usually in the Plain of Mars, are noticed elsewhere.

THE MOUNT OF THE MOON, in the lower part of the palm, opposite the Mount of Venus, tells us of the indefinite fancies and the disposition to reveries. The Moon favorable indicates fancy, sentimentality, love of mystery, love of solitude and of nature in quiet moods, vague desires, meditation, chastity, harmony in music, transcendental speculations, &c. In excess the Mount of the Moon will suggest caprice, unregulated fancies, sadness, irritation, excessive discontent, causeless despair, superstition, fanaticism. Its absence or depression is a lack of fancy, inelastic thoughts, a matter-of-fact person, dull imagination.

116 MOUNTS OF THE HAND.

Curved or tortuous lines on the Mount of the Moon show a restless and changeful fancy, and hence travels; a love of the mysterious and indefinite, hence contemplation, solitary habits and melancholy ideas.

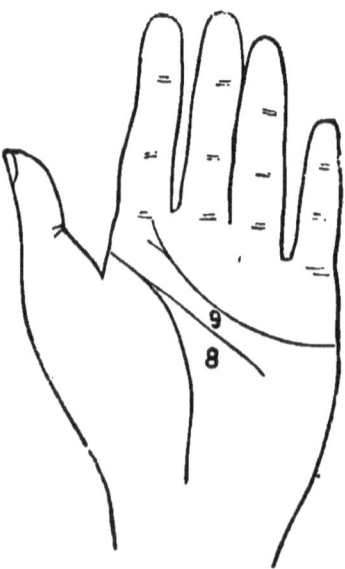

LOCALITIES—Triangle, [8] Quadrangle, [9]

THE TRIANGLE lies in the hollow of the hand, and is bounded by the vital, thought and assimilation lines, retaining its name even when the angles are not closed or the assimilation line is wanting.

The triangle of good size, bounded by well drawn lines, shows good health, lofty views, a nobility and boldness of character.

A small triangle is suggestive of weakness, pusillanimity, avarice and obstinacy. The skin of the triangle wrinkled is an unfavorable indication.

A well-defined and closed triangle formed by the thought, assimilation and material lines, shows a love of speculative thoughts, spiritual interests, natural magic and occult matters generally.

THE SUPREME ANGLE formed between the thumb and index finger by the union of the vital and thought lines, when clear and well-traced shows a good disposition—a delicate and noble nature. This angle obtuse suggests a dull perception. The two lines uniting below the mount of Saturn or lower in the hand, suggests extreme avarice, fearful forebodings of want, and a plodding, routine life. Confused lines in this angle suggest a gambler and voluptuary.

THE RIGHT ANGLE, formed by the union of the vital or material line with the assimilation, if well colored and fairly drawn, shows good health and good nature. The angle too sharp suggests weakened health and penuriousness. Too blunt or obtuse, and especially if the lines are not clear, suggests impaired health, rudeness and indolence.

THE LEFT ANGLE, formed by the union of the thought and assimilation lines, favorable, shows a strong nervous system and hence an effective active person. This angle too sharp shows a nervous temperament — irritable and unprincipled. Too obtuse it shows dullness of mind and inconstancy of purpose.

THE QUADRANGLE, also called the Table of the hand, lies between the thought and impulse lines. A broad Quadrangle, increasing in space towards the sides of the hand, indicates a good constitution, control of the emotions and passions — a loyal, faithful, happy person. Narrow, shows the opposite. When furrowed by numerous lines, especially cutting each other, a weak hand.

The quadrangle absent on account of a lacking impulse or thought line is a hint of uneven temper, bad disposition, wickedness, misfortune.

CHAPTER VII.

THE LINES OF THE HAND.

THE palm of the hand is traced with lines. These lines play an important part in all systems of "hand-reading." The ancients studied the lines of the hand long before they paid any attention to the mounts. The gipsies now give their palmistic divinations mainly from the lines. These lines have, like the mounts, been dedicated to the principal deities, and, in later days, to the planets. These names, as well as those of a more strictly fortune-telling character, are not only inappropriate, but most of them are misleading. The names adopted and used in this work, will, it is hoped, be somewhat an index to the real meaning and value of these " signatures " of man's life, health, impulses and peculiar mental endowments.

Besides several well defined and prominent lines, the palm usually presents numerous less conspicuous lines and marks. Even a slight examination, of any pair of hands, will show, as elsewhere stated, that the lines in one hand are not like those in the other; a careful comparison will often prove that no one line is exactly like its fellow — in the other hand. This variation of the lines of the hand is more fully described under the heading of "*Right and Left Hands.*"

In the lines of the hand, which vary in numerous particulars, the following peculiarities must be carefully observed:

Their place and position, in the hand in general, and in reference to the other lines and mounts;

Their length, breadth and depth, which are all variable, even in the same hand;

Their shape, as to straightness, curves, crookedness; whether they are uniform, regularly tapering, or abruptly different in form and quality. Lines may be gross, medium or weak;

Their color or complexion. In this it is to be observed whether they are alike or different, and whether each one is uniform, gradually changing, or abruptly spotted. The lines are of different shades in different persons, in the same person at different periods of life, and in different stages of health;

Their action, as bearing towards, touching,

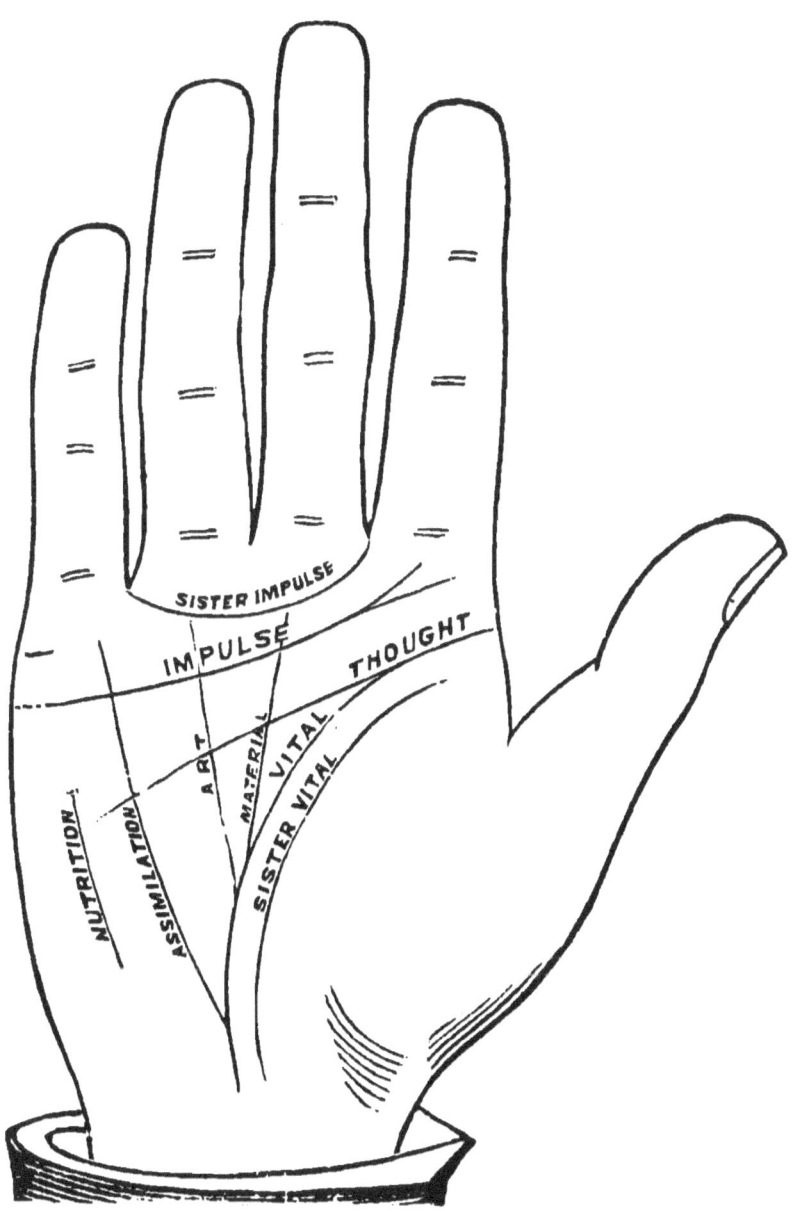

or traversing the mounts ; also in reference to the other lines, as approaching, touching, uniting with, crossing or cutting them; and whether the line cut or crossed is simply parted, or whether the severed ends are also displaced, so that the broken ends are not exactly opposite;

Their development, as to whether, in cutting or crossing another line, the direction of the cutting line is changed or its size or complexion altered;

Their passivity in relation to the other lines, as to being approached, touched, united with or cut by them, and whether when they are touched or cut they are also changed in size, color or direction.

The lines all vary in the above particulars. Some of them — even of the principal lines — may be entirely wanting, or so displaced as to be readily missed or easily mistaken for other lines, unless very carefully examined.

The lines are favorable as they are (1) in due location ; (2) long ; (3) clear; (4) well colored ; (5) straight or nicely curved; (6) even or gently tapering ; (7) beautified by graceful, well-defined, tapering branches ; (8) as they are united with, touched, or nearly approached by benefiting main or accidental lines.

MODIFICATION OF LINES.

The lines may be modified from the ideally perfect, through all the changes, to the extreme of opposite meaning by being (1) out of place; (2) indistinct or muddy; (3) badly colored, being too red or pale, or dark, either as a whole, in parts or in spots; (4) by abrupt or ungraceful changes of direction; (5) by sudden changes of size or depth; (6) by being disfigured by scraggy, ill-looking branches; (7) by being cut, approached by or united with unfavorable main or accidental lines.

A hand exhibiting many lines shows one mentally active, and if the lines are confused and interlacing will tell of unrest, perplexity, agitation of mind, irritation, fretfulness, etc.

THE VALUE OF THE VITAL LINE must be kept constantly in mind while interpreting all the other lines, singly or in their various combinations.

The hands of many laborers are smooth with few lines; not because their work has worn out the lines, but because their mental activity or disquietudes have never written them in the palm.

THE LINES DISAGREEING, but being equally clear and evenly colored, shows an even and regular change or growth in character. For particulars of this see *"Right and Left Hands."*

THE LINES IN THE TWO HANDS AGREEING, that is, being alike in general character and position, length and color, attest evenness of health and character.

THE PRINCIPAL LINES.

THE VITAL LINE, also called the Cardiaca, Temporalis, Dextræ-Trianguli, and Line of Life, rises at the edge of the palm, between the thumb and index finger, encloses the base of the thumb or mount of Venus, separating it from the palm of Mars and the mount of the Moon, and terminates at or near the wrist.

This line, as its name implies, and as its location in the lower part of the palm also suggests, especially represents the vitality of the individual — his constitution, condition of health, amount of energy, &c. It is, also, a record of at least the more severe past illness, and shadows forth the liability to the future development of disease. That is, it publishes such sickness or accidents as have left an unhealed damage upon the constitution, and also shows taints which may be developed into actual ailments.

The vital line and the mount of Venus are, therefore, the keys by which to interpret the physical condition and character of the per-

THE VITAL LINE. 125

son, and their meaning and value must be ever in the mind of the reader. Intellect, emotion, and even affection are, in this life any way, inhabitants of the physical man, and while they are not based upon the body, they are souled within it, and are therefore, modified in their power, purity and activity by that body and its condition of strength, energy and health.

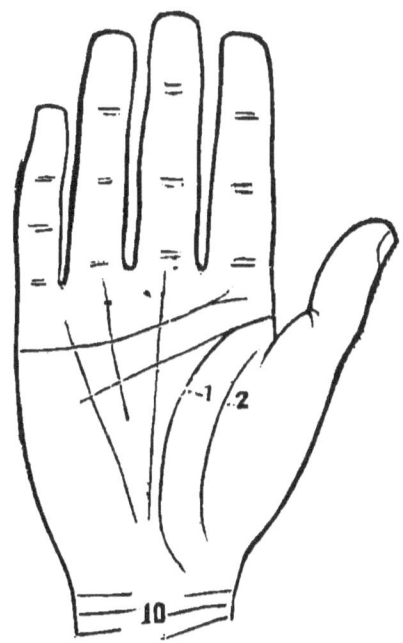

INES—Vital [1]. Sister Vital [2].

The vital line clearly drawn and well-formed, gently-colored, without breaks or cuts, and continuing completely round the mount of Venus until it unites with the wrist line, announces vigorous health, good constitution, freedom from dangerous or troublesome diseases, and, consequently, promises long life.

If this line is double, or if it is accompanied by a sister line, it shows a still more vigorous existence. The sister line repairs the defects of the main line. But if both the main and sister lines are weak, then the indications are worse. This line long and slender indicates low vitality and doubtful health. If this slender line is red it suggests excitement and irritability of temperament. If it is pale it shows slow movement of the blood, lack of strength and energy, and little endurance. This line broad and pale usually signifies a tendency to diseases of the stomach or other digestive and assimilating organs. The line broad and livid tells of weak and irregular circulation of the blood, and a tendency to disease of the heart.

This line badly formed, especially splintered or chained, is an indication of painful and troublesome diseases, suggesting disreputable ailments.

This line, cut by many little lines, suggests numerous sicknesses, capillary lines showing nervous troubles, headache, vertigo, &c.

The vital line indexes the health and ener-

DIVISION OF THE VITAL LINE.

gy not only in general, but to some extent, at least, in the particulars of health. While the present bodily condition is shown, the more severe sicknesses passed through leave their record on this line. Whether all illnesses are recorded or not is an open question, but it is pretty well established that any illness which has left an unhealed injury or a permanent change in the constitution, also leaves a permanent mark on the vital line. This mark is clear as the change is radical and yet abiding — and is at least dimmed as the weakness or change is overcome, and is probably obliterated from the hand as the system regains fully its normal condition. It is well known that many diseases, even when entirely cured, leave a radical and permanent change in the constitution. Such diseases also leave an indellible record on the vital line.

The age at which any sickness or accident occurred that has left an unhealed injury, or permanent effect upon the constitution, (and according to the ancient palmisters, the age at which any sickness or accident is threatened,) may be approximately determined by the location of the cut, break or change recording it, on the vital line.

The vital line is divided into decades, as follows:—

128 LINES OF THE HAND.

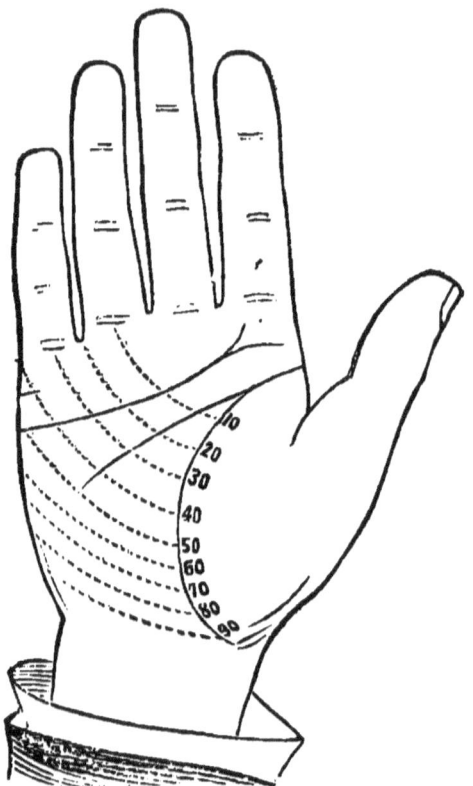

VITAL LINE—Marking the Decades of Life.

Take a pair of compasses, set the fixed point on the middle of the root of the index finger as a center, extend the movable point to the middle of the root of the third finger. Draw the arc of a circle, and mark this distance off on the vital line. That part of the line between the east edge of the hand and the point thus marked will represent the first ten years of the life. Next, extend the movable point to the division between the third and fourth finger, and this distance marked off on the vital line will note the twentieth year of life, and, hence, the space between the first and second markings will be the life between the tenth and twentieth years. The movable point extended to the middle of the fourth finger — to the edge of the hand at the root of the little finger — to the percussion of the palm where it is touched by the impulse line — will respectively give, when marked off on the vital line, the thirtieth, fortieth and fiftieth years. Measure off on the percussion of the hand below the impulse line, two-thirds of the distance between the root of the little finger and the impulse line, extend the movable point of the compass to this point and mark the distance off on the vital line for the sixtieth year. For each successive ten years take two-thirds of the distance given to the next preceding decade. Cuts or breaks in the vital line, suggest sickness or injury at the age shown, according to this measurement, and the division will repay close attention and careful study.

Since the vital line especially represents the physical condition of the person, and since much of the character, temperament and life depends upon the physical, this line is, therefore, an index also of much character. Temperament depends upon a combination of several characteristics, among which the vital line shows as follows:

The line broad and red shows a choleric temperament — violence and cruelty; depth and length add to this value and suggest fury. Decrease in size or color shows a corresponding modification.

The sanguine temperament is shown by a vital line long, clear, moderate size, and warm color, with branches at the beginning. A heightening of color and increase of branches intensifies the sign, and a toning down of the shade towards a citrine subdues the value of the line and suggests bilious temperament.

The line long, weak and pale indicates the phlegmatic temperament.

The line broad and pale, especially if it be short, broken, cut, or of a leaden hue, shows melancholy temperament.

The vital line usually begins at the edge of the palm about midway between the root of the thumb and the root of the first finger, sweeps with a moderate curve around the mount of Venus, dividing the lower palm into two nearly equal parts, the mount of

Venus and the mount of the Moon. Its location will repay careful attention, for any change from this ideal position is full of meaning.

As its beginning is carried towards the mount of Jupiter, it shows that mount to control the life and its uses, and hence tells of the ideal, theoretical and poetical bias, depending on the rest of the hand. As the beginning is carried down towards the thumb, it will indicate a life controlled by sensuous, passional or sensual instincts.

As the line passes near the mount of Venus especially if Venus crowd it into the middle of the hand, it will intensify the last characteristic which is likewise increased as it bends towards the thumb in passing to the wrist. As the line in passing towards the wrist curves far out into the plain of Mars it shows resolute and successful control of the passions. As it leans towards, or throws out branches upon the mount of the Moon, it will indicate a dreamy, uncertain, fanciful activity.

Branches rising from this line towards, upon or over the mount of Jupiter indicate ambition, with the life, energy and will bent for its attainment, and hence suggest ambition, ability, success, honor, distinction.

All branches *ascending* from this line are favorable, as they show aspirations toward elevated objects and ideals — the physical powers subordinated to the intellectual and emotional. They must be interpreted by the character of the mounts toward which they tend. All branches *descending* from the vital line are unfavorable, as indicating the rule of the sensuous nature and animal instincts.

The lower end — towards the wrist — bifurcated or branched is unfavorable as it shows the life worried by contending passions and unregulated fancies.

This line connected with the thought line signifies the life and the thought in harmony. Connected for a long distance will therefore point out a mind bound down to the material plane. As they are separated it shows a lack of unity between the idealities and the acts of life. If the space between them is filled with branches and interlacing lines it shows irritation and perplexity with one's self and condition, and suggests a struggle between the opposing elements of character — a subjective conflict — which will often place the person in trouble of mind and self-condemnation, and hint at changing moods, variable temper and vacillating purposes. As the space is clear and full it shows a calmer division of the mental and physical sides of life. This open space always shows impulsive

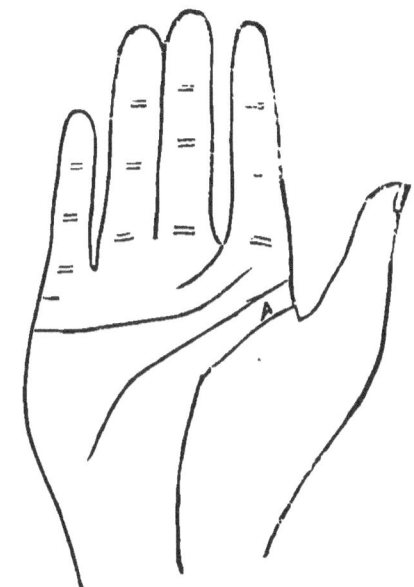

LINES—Vital and Thought Separated [A].

frankness, and suggests eccentricity, ideality and sensuous sensitiveness. In a hand otherwise good it suggests confidence in one's self, dislike of restraint, and, consequently, love of independence, love of ruling, and faithfulness in service. In an undeveloped hand this open space indicates an instinctive life, running its course without guidance from the judgment, hence the plodder — the hewer of wood, drawer of water, shoveler of dirt. In a weak hand it suggests folly, vanity, envy, irritation, unhappy repining, melancholy, falsehood, disgrace. If with this space the vital and thought lines are strong and red and, especially if the impulse line is unfavorable, there is shown passion and intensity running riot without intellectual control; hence, violence, cruelty, brutality, vulgarity and obscenity — still worse if the thought and affection lines unite.

This separation of the vital and thought lines may suggest the inspired seer, who in ecstatic rapture soars in the warm empyrean of spiritual contemplation. while he dwells without strong protest in the midst of sin and suffering. It may announce the calm philosopher, surveying truth in the white light of perception, crucifying his appetites, and foregoing his bodily comforts, for the sake of pure thinking. It belongs to the absent-minded man, who in his thought wanders far from his work; to the theorist who seldom if ever materializes his ideas; to the genius, who suggests wonderful inventions or improvements upon which other men build fortunes; it suggests the versatile and accomplished bohemian, who is the master critic who sees and feels every delicacy of shade in the good, the true and the beautiful, but who frequently lacks the industry, or continuity, or self-valuation to unify the life into the grand possibility of achievement. These are the bright possibilities of this striking peculiarity of the hand, and the shadows are correspondingly dark on the unfortunate plane. This separation of the vital and thought lines often belongs to the hypocrite, who lives one life and pretends another; to the enthusiast, who writes of the beauties of virtue and revels in the bestial excesses of debauchery. It is found in the hand of the clergyman who separates doctrine and life, and also to him who disgraces his sacred calling. It is very common in the hand of that class of abandoned women who are elegant in manners, refined in appearance, attractive by graces of mind and culture: who understand the beauty of holiness and recognize the worth of virtue, and yet lead a life which they at once detest and idolize; mingling with men whom they at the same time admire and despise. From all of this and much more that might be said, we find the real meaning of the open space between the vital and thought lines to be, that there is a lack of harmony, and usually little real connection between the impulses of the heart, the thoughts of the brain, and the acts of the life. As this open space separates these lines the thought line is carried towards the mount of Jupiter, while the vital line approaches the root of the thumb, or the mount of Venus. This shows ideality, imagination, ambition in the thoughts, while the life is modified or controlled by the sensuous and animal propensities. It is all-important to decide which "carries it over the other" — thought or passion, reflection or emotion, ideas or impulse. The one opens to truth and virtue, wisdom and goodness, perception and inspiration; the other to passion, impulse and sensuality. It is often that the one or the other alternately rules, and then we have the conflict of the two, and the person is of that peculiar character which many like and few fully endorse — of whom it is so frequently said, "He means well — but —"; "She is fascinating and good — but —"; or who is like the little girl who,

"When she is good is very, very good
And when she is bad she is horrid."

The vital line united with the thought line and at the same time with the impulse line is usually an undesirable combination. This union shows a mingling of the emotions, thought and activity that is unprofitable. Like the last, it is either very good or very bad, always denoting a very peculiar person

— oftentimes a dangerous character. One with the lines thus united will generally mingle the feelings with the thoughts and life so as to make a personal application of every agreement or disagreement; so as to think well of those who agree with him or who commend his action, and to dislike those who disagree with him in thought, word or action. So he defends his friends at all hazards and denounces his enemies, or those whom he dislikes, on all occasions. Those who agree with him are saints and philosophers. Those

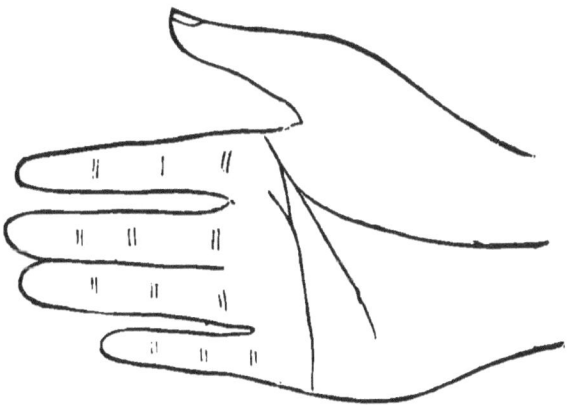

who differ are knaves or fools. The good side of this union of the vital, thought and impulse lines is that the man will make his life as pure, and his thoughts as clear as his ideals.

The vital line uneven in size, changing in

direction, and varied in color, shows uncertain health and liability to irritation, quarreling and violence. The vital line frequently tapers and comes to an end before reaching the wrist, while the material line starts from the wrist full and clear, tapering as it ascends, almost touching, sometimes uniting with, the vital; thus replacing the lower end of the latter line. This is found in the hands of him who is good for counsel, or for plan, but who dislikes the drudgery of execution.

The vital line bifurcated near the wrist suggests brain troubles, insanity, dementia. The

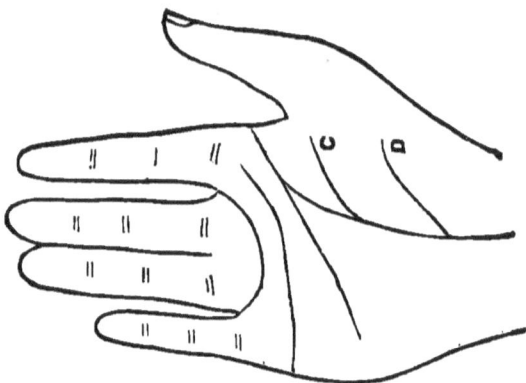

vital line sending a branch [C] out towards the junction of the thumb with the palm on the east edge of the hand, suggests one easily duped by fascinating and designing women.

A branch [D] leaving the vital line near the

THE VITAL LINE. 139

wrist and running off towards the thumb suggests dissipation and lewdness.

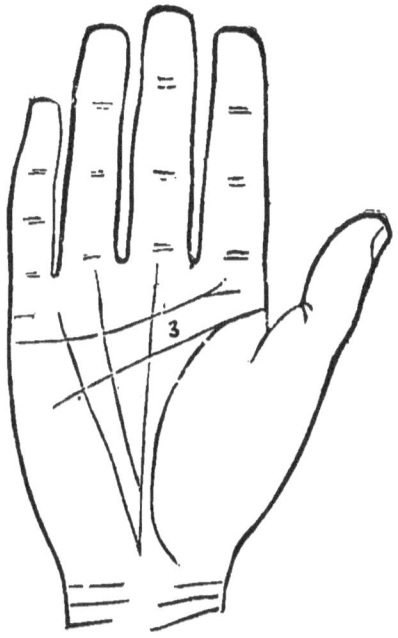

Lines –Thought [3].

THE THOUGHT LINE, also called the Cephalica, Cerebri Vivifica Prosperitas, Sinistra Trianguli, Line of the Head and Natural Line — begins at or near the edge of the hand, between the thumb and the index finger, traverses the plain of Mars, separating the triangle from the quadrangle of the hand, and usually ends on the mount of Mars, or curves down upon or over the mount of the Moon.

This line favorable, clearly united with the

vital line, following a direct or slightly downward curving course, signifies a lucid mind working in a healthy brain ; hence clear perception, sound judgment, and a strong will. Passing through the plain of Mars and to, upon or through the mount of Mars, its character must be interpreted by the peculiarity of those localities. These localities favorable show calmness and power with which to meet all opposition and struggles, using, without abusing or fearing, what the fates present — the opportunities and accidents of life.

A good sister line is very favorable. For the meaning of the thought line, when united to or separated from the vital line, see page 132.

If the line continues straight through the palm and well over the mount of Mars it marks a disposition to concentration — the putting forth of one's thoughts and efforts on some one line of study, occupation or work. It also announces a good memory. Other signs accompanying it may announce the specialist in philosophy, science or business. It suggests — by its calculation and concentration — the specialist, the hobbyist, the fanatic, the enthusiast; economy and avarice,

THE THOUGHT LINE.

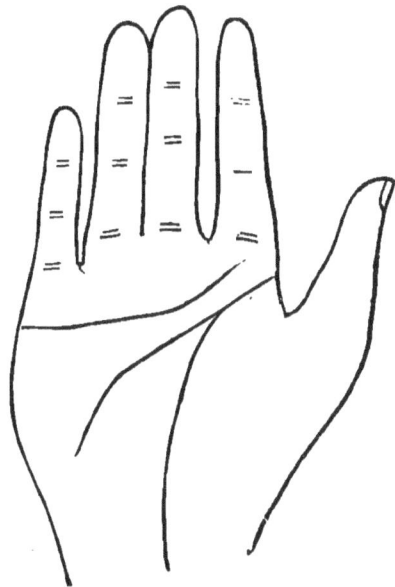

This line curving down on the mount of the Moon suggests fanciful projects, changeable plans, capricious views, unregulated and visionary causes of conduct, extravagant and artificial ideas of life, romance, liberality, prodigality, mysticism. This is all increased as the line continues straight through the plain of Mars, and then suddenly turns down on the mount of the Moon; and as the end of the line extends towards the lower part of the mount, near the wrist; also as the character of that mount carries the same meaning. The thought line making a clear cross with the assimilation line has the same general meaning — intensifying the above.

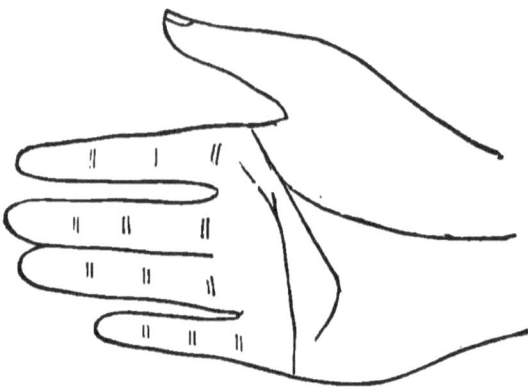

If this line tends upwards towards the impulse line it indicates that the emotions bias the thoughts and plans, especially as to the qualities of the mounts towards which it tends. A moderate rise, in graceful curves, shows the thoughts warmed by the affections.

Branches rising from the thought line have the same meaning—less intense. Branches falling from the thought-line are unfavorable, both as indicating disease of the brain or nerves, and as showing erratic and unsound thinking.

If this line, or its branches, touch or unite with the impulse line—especially if the latter is cut, and particularly if the severed ends are also displaced—its interpretation will partake of the bad indications of the mount under which the affection line is touched or cut. (See page 148.) This line formed like a chain shows inability to fix one's ideas; suggests insanity, and is one of the marks of an imbecile. This line long, slender, and pale, suggests a weak brain, and hints at untruthfulness, infidelity, unfaithfulness, treason, &c.

As the line is short it suggests a weak will; broad and shallow, lack of concentration; pale, little intellectual force, lack of circumspection; deep, malevolence; too red, anger, violence, apoplexy.

This line bifurcated on the mount of Mars, one branch going straight onward and the other descending on the mount of the Moon, shows an apprehension of the practical side of life, and a tendency to fancy, romance and mysticism. One branch of the thought line rising towards the impulse line and another descending on the mount of the Moon will suggest self-deception, quaint ideas, separation of theory and practice, invention of plots, mimicry, falsehood, hypocrisy.

This line ending or cut under Saturn is unfavorable.

This line tortuous or eneven shows a vacillating disposition and suggests weakness, anger, presumption, theft — general unreliability.

A branch or branches arising from the thought line and passing straight or gracefully curved upon or over Jupiter, announces a disposition or ability to utilize the imagination in a thoughtful, successful manner. If this branch, however, rise under Saturn and penetrate the first finger, it suggests vanity and selfishness.

Points or dots on this line suggest brain troubles; red — rush of blood to the head, nervous agitation or irritation — arbitrary opinions, violent passions, sudden bursts of temper; sometimes, brilliant perceptions, originality and invention, etc.; white — weak nerves, depleted brain, fainting fits, vertigo — depressed spirits, dull thoughts, etc.

THE IMPULSE LINE, also called the Mensalis, Necessaria, Martis, Vesicalis, Renalis, Thoralis, Generativa, Epidemica, Pestifera, Table Line, Line of Fortune and Line of the Heart, begins at the percussion of the hand, under the mount of Mercury, traverses the palm towards the east, separating the mounts of the hand from the Quadrangle and usually terminating at, passing upon, or traversing the mount of Jupiter.

This line favorable, commencing in proper place, clearly drawn, well colored, gracefully curved, extending fairly upon the mount of Jupiter, clearly and gracefully branched at the terminations — indicates warm emotions,

THE IMPULSE LINE. 145

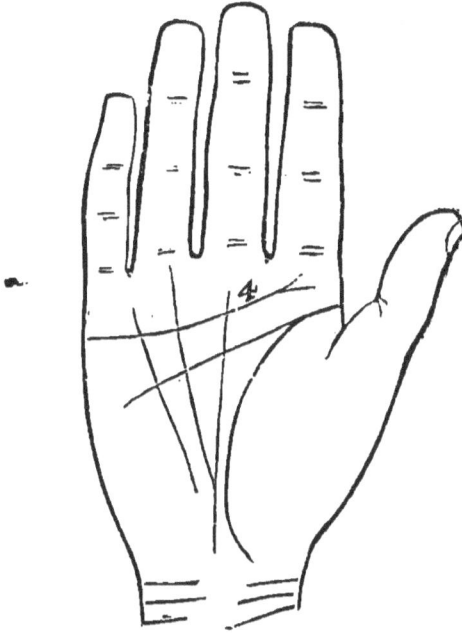

LINES--Impulse [4].

generous nature, unselfish disposition, strong friendships, ardent affection, permanent attachments — all intensified as the line extends over the mount of Jupiter. If it pass to the edge of the hand under the index finger it shows intense love and tenderness, suggesting great happiness or misery — perhaps these alternately — in affairs of the heart.

This line passing over the mount of Jupiter to the edge of the hand and seeming to curl round the index finger — known to ancient palmisters as the " Ring of Solomon "— suggests ideal attachments, romantic adventures, self-sacrifice for the loved one. It thus suggests one who will sing —

"Amazing brightness, purity, and truth,
Eternal joy, and everlasting love,"

and in the opposite mood, the heart all dark and the perceptions dimmed, will wail, shedding floods of —

" Tears from the depths of some divine despair."

This line terminating between the index and middle finger, or under that position, indexes a tranquil, rational, steady affection — an even life. Terminating under the middle finger shows a selfish bias to the love relations; this attachment may be strong — but the suggestion is of one who desires to be loved rather than love, ministered to rather than minister, to have his wishes gratified rather than sacrifice for another, to be looked up to, asked for direction, obeyed. Ending under the third finger attests a sordid as well as a selfish foundation for the feelings, and hints that any true love or genuine friendship is improbable, if not impossible, and suggests one who thinks of —

"Gratitude as a lively sense of future favors."

This line terminating under the little finger or absent, indicates lack of sympathy, coldness of nature, bad faith, aptness for evil, cruelty. This line showing a serpentine course suggests an unreliable, faithless person, especially in dealings with the opposite sex.

This line and the thought line sometimes run into each other in such a way as to pre-

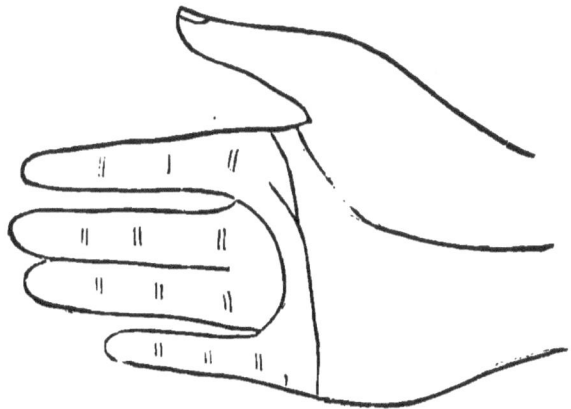

sent only one line — clear or ragged — across the hand, suggesting a person who — especially if the thumb is weak and the palm full or hard — will be ruled by his emotions and his thoughts in turn; the character will be uneven, therefore, governed by feeling without the light or guidance of thought or reason; or, on the other hand, by cool calculation and logic devoid of emotion or affection. The thought or the impulse, whichever first gets control, will in each case rule without the beneficent coöperation of the other, and the person will be at one time all feeling, at another all calculation — tender or cruel, thoughtful or careless. This is further intensified if the vital and thought lines are not united under the index finger. (See page 132.)

The impulse and thought lines both present in the hand and united have a special value which should be interpreted by the unfavorable character of the mount under which they meet. Meeting under Jupiter will suggest inordinate ambition, under Saturn, melancholy; under Apollo, vanity, selfishness, love of riches; under Mercury, dishonesty, theft, crime.

Breaks — or cuts by other than the principal lines, especially if the severed ends are also displaced, are unfavorable; cuts suggest an outside influence, breaks index a subjective cause for the undesirable characteristics shown. Cuts or breaks under Saturn hint at fatality, selfishness, melancholy; between that and Apollo, folly; under the latter, vanity; between Apollo and Mercury, avarice; under Mercury, ignorance, pretension, incapacity, dishonesty. Breaks in this line often suggest impotency; for this compare the mount of Venus and the vital line.

Branches of this line on Jupiter, if not too

numerous or ill-shapen, are favorable. If rising gracefully from this line, they are indications of the favor of the mount to which they tend. Ill-shapen or broken branches take the faults of such mounts. Branches falling towards the thought line indicate a much modified meaning of the union of the two lines — a conflict between reason and impulse — duty and affection.

This line bare of branches in a good hand, shows concentration of affection on one person or pursuit; in a cold nature it indicates selfishness—lack of tenderness, sympathy, or affection.

This line chained, or with short stubbed branches, or made up of fine capillary strands — especially if they are overlapping instead of continuous — in the order named — shows lack of concentration in the ideals or objects of affection, and suggests coquetry, flirtations, instability, inconstancy, love intrigues.

This line, as it is long, shows constancy and tenderness; as it is large, strength of feeling, which near the percussion of the hand will suggest an amorous and sensuous bias, and near the termination an ideal and sentimental tendency. As it is broad it shows dissipation of energy; as it is red, intensity; pale, weakness of impulse or feeling.

Spots or knots on this line suggest abrupt, sudden and violent emotions, especially in relation to the opposite sex; red, if intense anger, grief, jealousy, revenge; white, hints at cowardice, fear and selfishness.

The absence of this line shows a cold nature and suggests, as the vital line or mount of Venus may corroborate, one impotent, or a eunuch.

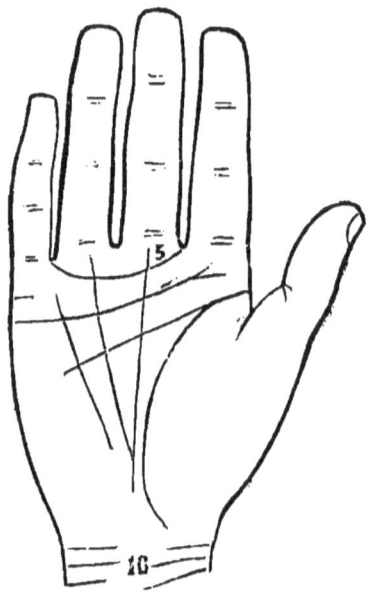

Lines—Sister Impulse, [5]

THE SISTER IMPULSE LINE, when present in the hand, is drawn between the impulse line and the roots of the fingers. Its usual location is to begin between the little and third fingers, inclosing or traversing the mounts of Apollo and Saturn and terminating between the middle and index fingers.

This line has usually been called the Girdle of Venus, and palmisters have heretofore, without exception, given it only a sensuous, impure or disgraceful meaning. It is, however, a sister, or supplementary, to the impulse line, and should, therefore, be interpreted by the character and value of the latter — the meaning of which it intensifies and deepens.

This line indicates vehement yet delicate impulses, appetites and passions; showing one who loves all that is sensuously beautiful, brilliant, exciting and intense; and suggests one who will at once minister to the appetites and passions under the impulse of feeling rather than under the guidance of thought. With these ardent passions and delicate sensibilities regenerated and purified, this line may show ideal delicacy, fervid purity and enthusiastic self-sacrifice for others.

This line doubled is thereby intensified.

One with this line will always have a peculiar, and, in some respects, an unevenly developed character.

This line tortuous, broken, or cut by accidental lines, shows irritation and contention of impulses, and suggests impurity, refined and brilliant profligacy, voluptuous debauchery, gilded depravity, artistic obscenity — never low or filthy vulgarity. One end leaning towards Mercury shows one who loves finesse, intrigue, love-making, etc., but can, if he will, control his appetites. Traversing

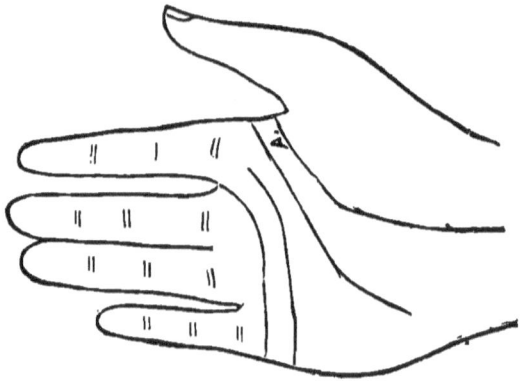

Mercury and ending at the root of the little finger, suggests depraved licentiousness, using falsehood, artifice or force to secure its victims, and hints strongly at theft and swindling.

SECONDARY LINES.

THE MATERIAL LINE, also called the line of Saturn, Line of Fate, and (when broken, distorted' or much cut) Via Combusta, may

THE MATERIAL LINE. 153

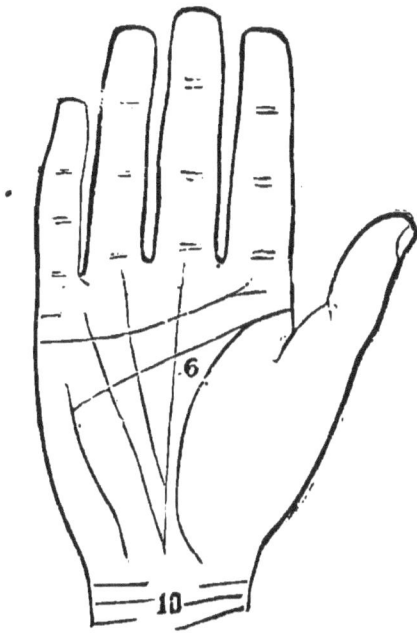

LINES—Material, [6]

originate almost anywhere in the lower part of the palm. Its base is usually found on the vital line, in the plain of Mars, or on the mount of the Moon. Its general course is towards the mount of Saturn, near or upon which it generally ends.

The ideally favorable material line is one which rises near the wrist, in close proximity to a good vital line, passes clearly and directly on, gracefully closing in a single, double or triple termination, on the highest part of a clear and favorable mount of Saturn. Such a line attests a practical, industrious, happy person who will intelligently and successfully employ his abilities and opportunities to attain his favorite object and position in life.

The material line always partakes of the character and meaning of the line or locality from which it starts. Rising on the vital line it partakes of the value of that line, showing, too, the work of life based on practical and material foundations, and that the life and character is much governed by the sensuous and vital peculiarities of the man. Rising on or near the wrist, luxuriant natural ability

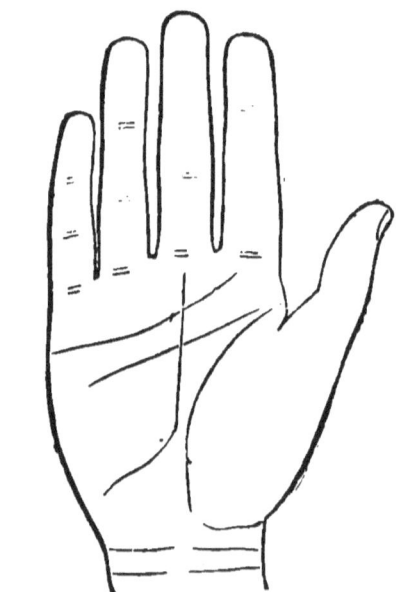

and untiring industry. Rising on the mount of the Moon indicates a life much guided or

THE MATERIAL LINE. 155

swerved by indefinite, fanciful or illy-defined plans. Rising in the mount of Venus tells of

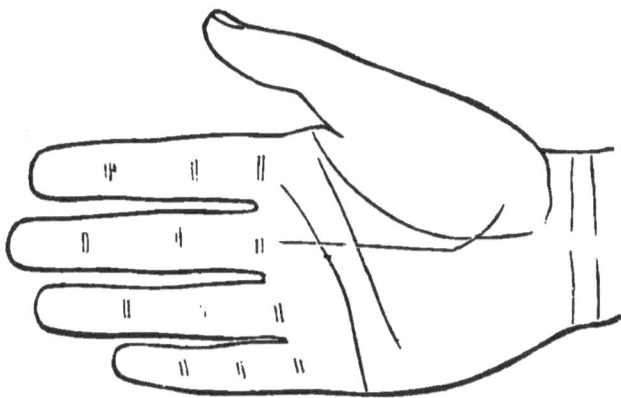

a strong sensuous bias to the life, and suggests excessive impurity. Rising in two

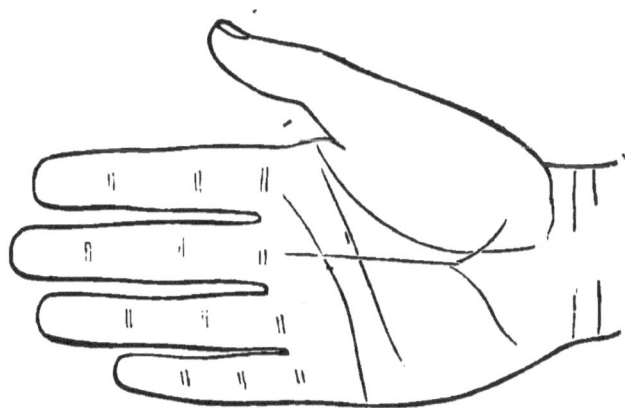

branches, one on the mount of Venus and the other on the mount of the Moon, and uniting in the hollow of the hand, indicates strong sensual power and intensity, with wild and impure imagination, suggesting gross lewdness, selfishness and malevolence. Rising in the plain of Mars, suggests a plodding, busy, routine worker, who bears bravely the ills he cannot overcome. Rising on the mount of Mars tells of an aggressive, battling, defiant character who will attempt, at least, to overcome all opposition, and in a weak hand shows the braggart, petty tyrant, and parade soldier. Rising at the thought line indicates one whose life and plans have an intellectual object — philosophy, logic, science. Beginning at the impulse line it suggests one whose life is for the sake of his affections, impulses, or emotions; one whose plans are founded in and controlled by his loves and friendships.

The line straight or very moderately curved, shows directness of plan and promptness of execution — the effort well-directed and effective. The line tortuous shows conflict on the subjective side of life — a change of purpose or a division of energies. Cut or broken tells of one who has met serious obstacles which have frustrated his plans and annulled or overcome his efforts. This is especially attested if the line is also displaced at the points of the cuts or breaks; in the lower part of the palm it shows the battle to have been one with a sensuous, passional or imaginative foundation; as the line is near Venus or the Moon. Broken or cut and misplaced at the thought-

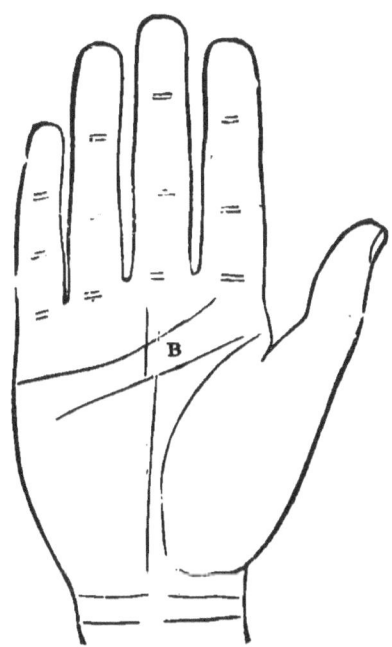

line (B) suggests one who makes many plans and easily changes them on reasonable ground, and hints at one who delights in plans but dislikes the routine or labor of execution — one who will work willingly, maybe enthusiastically, so long as the brain must be as active as the hand. The break or cut and

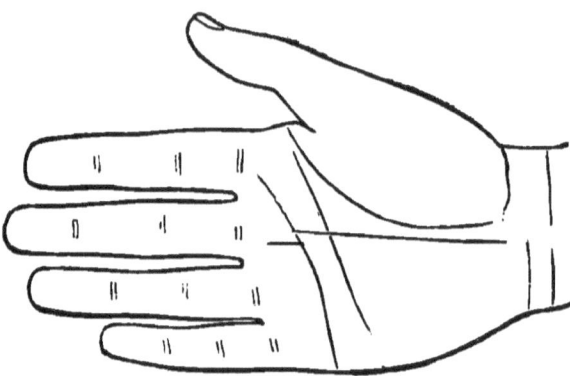

the misplacement occurring at the impulse line shows one whose plans are interfered with by his emotions and affections — suggesting disastrous love affairs, unfortunate intrigue, disgraceful inconstancy, as other tendencies may determine.

This line terminating clearly on the mount of Saturn is most favorable, as it shows the ideal plan and the expended effort to be in unison for the desired result. A division on this mount into two or three clear branches is desirable; muddy, indistinct, broken or ill-shapen branches, and the contrary in the order named. Terminating at the impulse line shows one whose feelings rule the life; one who is generally a favorite with the opposite sex; one whose plans, purposes and work must yield to his emotions — to love, friendship and humanity in the pure and true man — to impulse and appetite in the impure and unfaithful one. Terminating at the thought-line shows one who loves theory, meditation, logic; who willingly works out an idea or a plan, but who prefers not to do any merely manual work. Who is enthusiastic in developing and teaching any new idea or invention, but who considers his labor at an end when he has clearly finished the brain-work.

This line penetrating to the middle finger, shows a positive person who will persistently, obstinately, arbitrarily, tyrannically, follow his adopted course of action to obtain the goal sought, and besides one who will, consequently, meet with remarkable successes and failures.

This line tortuous, formed like a screw, or of various branches or broken parts, at the root suggests one who has worried and seen troublous experiences; if the line continues bad the character is the same; if, however, the line improves as it ascends, it shows the person to have overcome the subjective cause of the troubles and to be leading a comparatively tranquil and successful life.

A hand without this line will usually lack in executive ability, material success and personal influence.

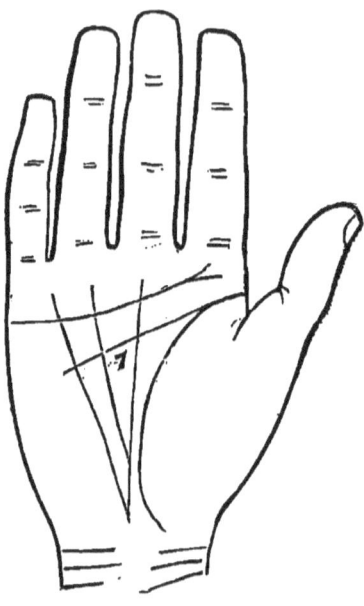

Lines--Art, [7].

THE ART LINE also known as the line of Apollo, and the Line of the Sun, may rise upon the Vital line, or anywhere between that and the percussion of the hand and proceeds towards or to the mount of Apollo. A favorable line is straight, clearly drawn, fairly colored, of medium size, and continues without breaks, cuts by accidental lines, or falling branches, through the mount of Apollo. It indicates a love of sensuous beauty, art, merit, riches, glory, fame, prominence, personal grandeur, according as other aptitudes are more or less developed.

It will suggest the sculptor, painter, poet, musician, singer, critic, practical scientist, inventor of machinery and industrial appliances, the superior artizan, as other characteristics may determine. In short, this line suggests one who readily and successfully, clearly and rapidly, puts his imaginations and inventions into practical and sensuous form. It indicates one who loves success through personal effort of brain and hand, one who desires recognition for personal worth of virtue, artistic merit, riches, beauty or show, either actual or assumed.

This line like the others, is modified in its meaning by the locality of its rise, course and termination. Rising from the vital line, it suggests a sensuous and material basis; and if it also terminates short of the middle of the mount hints at extreme lust. Its roots in the plain of Mars tells of a ready use of the offered opportunities; while coming from the mount of Mars will indicate one who forces even opposing obstacles into his own service. Rising on the mount of the Moon will strongly hint at fanciful plans, changing purposes, graceful but impractical accomplishments.

As this line is curved or undulating it will partake of the qualities of the localities to which it goes, or towards which it tends. As its termination leans towards Mercury there is a suggestion of personal persuasiveness through conversational powers, magnetic force, or eloquence; while a leaning towards Saturn is an indication of determined, persistent effort, or of fearful foreboding, and timidity of character, according as Saturn is clear or cloudy.

Lines attaching to, impeding or cutting this line, especially at its roots, suggest that obstacles objective are not readily overcome; while accidental lines, thwarting or cutting across this line on the mount of Apollo show serious subjective obstacles to success. This line passing into two equal branches shows power impaired and results modified by a division of effort — more plans than realizations. If the branches are unequal it suggests that the effort put forth has been mainly in one direction, while taste for other work still remains.

Three equal terminal branches are better than two — suggesting talent, industry and success; this is especially desirable if they branch at the impulse line, when it shows strength, warmth and purity of feeling — art enlivened and controlled by affection. Branching at the thought line shows clearness of perception, rational plans, with intelligent and effective application — art and industry lighted and guided by reason.

This line stronger below than on the mount suggests more plan, purpose and ideality than performance; while a line, light at the root, and stronger above — especially if it terminate abruptly before reaching the middle of the mount of Apollo — indicates the ardent effort of one not clear in his purpose. The art line terminating on Apollo in many fine and graceful branches — especially if the mount is also favorable — indicates intensity of artistic feeling and versatility of execution, but not great success in any one line. This line is often indistinct or lacking.

THE ASSIMILATION LINE, also called the Stomachi, Basis Trianguli, Hepatic, and Liver Line, begins in the lower part of the palm, on or near the vital line, or between that and the percussion of the hand, and ends near the table line under the mount of Mercury, on that mount, or at the root of the little finger.

The ideal assimilation line rises at the wrist, near but not upon the vital line, proceeds directly or in graceful undulations, being clearly drawn, of medium strength and fairly colored, through the plain of Mars and

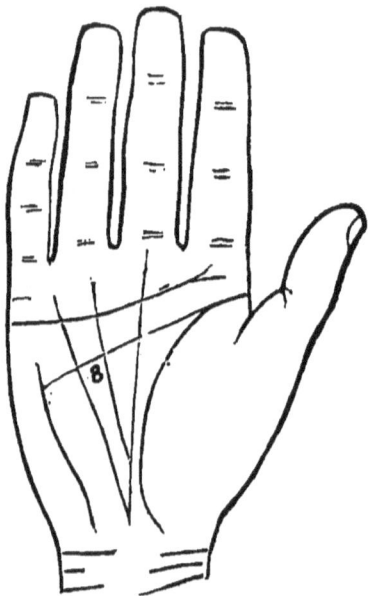

LINES—Assimilation [8].

mount of Mercury, and terminates on the upper part of that mount at the root of the little finger. Such a line tells of good digestion, good memory, love of humor and wit, happy views of life, gay spirits — hence a favorite in society, successful in business, a good conversationist, with diplomatic ability.

This line winding or tortuous shows bilious derangements, and, hence, melancholy temperament. This line broken or ragged tells of indigestion or dyspepsia, and suggests an uneven temper, irritability, fault-

THE ASSIMILATION LINE.

finding, &c. The line red shows strong appetite, violent craving, and, hence, anger, violence, coarseness. The line pale shows lack of assimilating power, low vitality, little energy, and will suggest listless thought, careless dress, lack of interest in the active pursuits of life.

This line of unfavorable character, rising on the vital line suggests heart-disease. Originating on the mount of the Moon hints at nervous or brain depletion, suggesting capricious health and fancied troubles.

This line rising on the mount of Venus and passing directly to the mount of Mercury well drawn and of good color, shows ardent love of sensuous beauty; strong passion; persuasiveness in conversation; success in love-making; and suggests the one loving and happy in marital relations; the graceful and favorite society gentleman; the fascinating gallant; the insinuating deceiver; the successful diplomat; the polished confidence operator; the accomplished swindler; depending on the other characteristics to direct how this personal presence and captivating address shall be used.

This line lacking, which is often the case, is more favorable than a poor or defective line present.

166 LINES OF THE HAND.

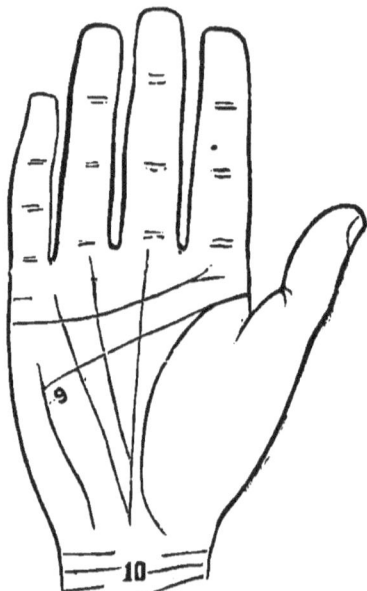

Lines—Nutrition [9]. Wrist [10].

THE NUTRITION LINE, also called the Milky Way, when found in the hand, traverses the mount of the Moon in a direction nearly parallel to the assimilation line, of which it is really a sister line. This line is the more favorable as it rises near the wrist and terminates at or near the mount of Mercury, telling of robust health. This line tells of strong and sentimental amative propensities, a love for and favor with the opposite sex, and suggests large families of healthy and much-loved children.

This line crooked or ill-shapen, or badly

colored, suggests the vital powers impaired from excessive indulgence, or depletion by disgraceful diseases.

THE WRIST LINES, also known as the Rascette and Discriminational lines, separate the hand from the arm by a "single, double or triple transcussion" at the wrist. These lines well-drawn and favorable indicate good health, a vigorous constitution, and a tranquil disposition. These lines in links or chains, suggest plodding and only partially enlightened labor. Falling down on the mount of the Moon, they show a love of travel and adventure — or in a weak hand a restless discontented person.

One line on the edge of the hand between the little finger and the impulse line and parallel with the latter, shows one strong in attachments, firm in friendship and devoted to the marital partner, home and children. Two or more lines similarly situated show one who, losing a friend, lover, or wedded companion will naturally replace them.

ACCIDENTAL LINES.

Accidental lines of numerous forms, as well as of varying importance, modify the meaning of the different main lines, mounts and localities upon or near which they are found in the hand.

BRANCHES are small lines, usually proceeding from the commencement or termination of the principal or secondary lines. Branches of good form rising from a main line add to the good qualities of that line, and to the good indications of the locality where found; while ill-shapen branches, or those falling downward from the main line, tell of the unfavorable characteristics of that line and detract from the value of the locality which they traverse.

Branches forming or tending to form chains indicate hindrances, contradictions and struggles between the good and bad qualities of the line.

AN ISLAND in a line suggests the temptation and strong inclination towards the evil use of the powers and aptitudes indicated by the line, and hints at injured health in consequence.

An island on the material line shows general sensual impurity; the part of the palm where found indicating its peculiar character.

On the vital line an island suggests brutal indulgences, lowering the vitality. On the thought line, in the plain of Mars, it gives a hint of a sanguinary disposition, cruelty, and of a rush of blood to the brain, in case of excitement or passion. On the thought line, in the quadrangle, it suggests shameful thoughts and love of prurient practices.

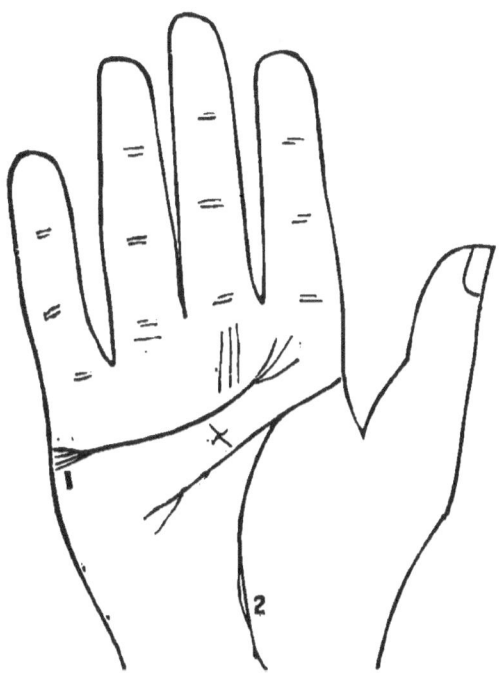

Lines—Branches [1]. Island [2].

An island on the impulse line shows impure impulses, temptations to voluptuous dissipation, and refined or elegant debauchery.

On the assimilation line, especially as it tends towards the mount of Mercury, an island will suggest deception, cheating, intrigue, theft, etc.

CAPILLARY LINES which unite to form a main line, indicate an impediment to effective action by dissipating the power in too many channels — irritation and activity without united action.

VERTICAL LINES.—All accidental lines, clearly drawn, well formed, straight or gracefully and slightly curved, and vertical in direction, add to the good qualities of the localities upon which they are impressed. This is especially true as they are single and of fair size, but diminishes as the number is increased, or as they dwindle in size or fail in beauty.

TRANSVERSE LINES. — Accidental lines crossing the mounts or cutting the main or minor lines, generally indicate characteristics which weaken, annul or overcome the aptitudes shown by the locality or lines traversed or cut. This adverse indication is increased as the lines are numerous and ill-shapen.

CURVED LINES show a swerving disposition.

CROOKED LINES show opposing forces hindering each other.

BROKEN LINES indicate lack of continuity of thought and action.

TORTUOUS LINES tell of opposing and changing purposes and opportunities; a deviating character.

GRILLS, that is, several lines crossing

ACCIDENTAL LINES. 171

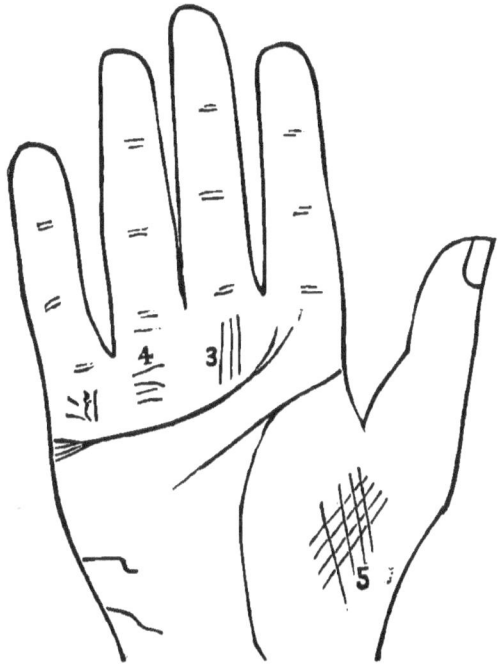

LINES—Vertical [3]. Transverse [4]. Grills [5].

and cutting each other like net-work, are generally undesirable, suggesting irritation, excitability and intensity of the qualities shown by the locality where found.

On the mount of Jupiter they suggest a tendency to superstition, egotism and vanity.

On the mount of Saturn, sad forebodings and fear of misfortune.

On the mount of Apollo, folly, error, desire of undeserved glory.

On the mount of Mercury, deception, lying, theft, petty intrigue and mischief-making.

On the mount of the Moon, inquietude, discontent, gloomy imaginations.

On the mount or plain of Mars, violent contentions, sudden or intense anger.

On the mount of Venus, unchastity, coarseness, vulgarity, obscenity.

CROSSES indicate an intensity and undue activity of the characteristics of the locality where found, without adding to its strength, and suggest irritation, sensitiveness, and unrest. This is especially true when the crosses are illy formed, of crooked or broken lines, or with unequal arms. Sometimes, however, a well formed cross is a very desirable accompaniment to other signs in the hand.

There are occasions when the intensity and unrest suggested by the cross, even when illy made, counterbalances some other defect.

A cross on the mount of Venus shows a tendency to sensuous excitement, and, therefore, suggests impurity, lasciviousness and obscenity. This is especially the case as the cross is found upon the lower part of the mount.

A cross in the base of the hand between the mount of Venus and the mount of the Moon shows one who has conflicts between passion and purity; suggesting that the sensuous and the ideal are in turn triumphant, and hints at a person who loves adventure and romance.

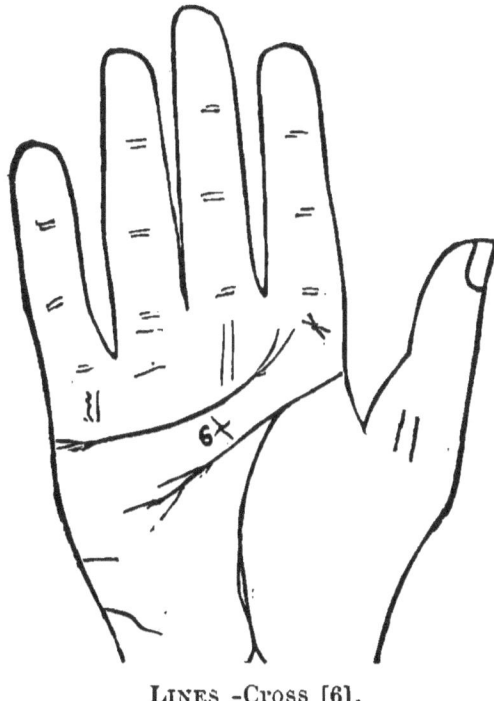

LINES -Cross [6],

A cross on the mount of the Moon, well formed indicates one who loves the mysterious and occult, with a lively but not well balanced fancy. The cross here, illy formed, hints at one who is often self-deceived and, hence, one who deceives others.

A cross in the plain of Mars tells of a person who vehemently opposes what is unpleasant, who is irritated and easily angered.

On the mount of Mars it asserts an actively aggressive disposition, which in an impulsive hand, will be dangerous; and in a philosophical one, coolly and persistently oppressive.

A cross on the mount of Jupiter is favorable and tells of warm and strong ideal attachments, and a genial and hearty disposition.

A cross on the mount of Saturn, sometimes called the "mystic cross," suggests an erratic and positive fatalism which produces strange results, good and bad.

A cross on the mount of Apollo hints at one whose aspirations towards, and love of art are brilliant, dazzling, confusing — one who gives promise of more than he can ultimate — one "whose abilities are believed in, not demonstrated."

A cross on the mount of Mercury suggests intrigue, deception, theft, robbery. In a weak hand, love of money, glitter, show. In a cold hand, sordid or miserly tendencies.

A cross in the quadrangle under Saturn suggests gloomy superstition; above Saturn, toward Jupiter, one likely to be the plaything of the beloved one of the opposite sex; under Mercury, successful travels and changeable life.

STARS are always interpreted as intensified

ACCIDENTAL LINES. 175

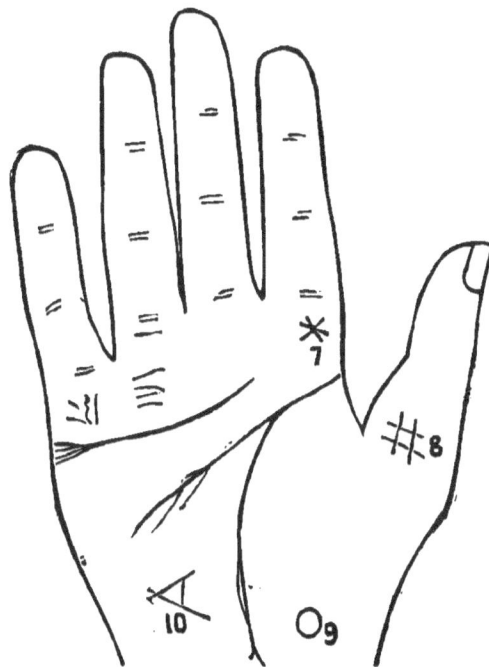

LINES—Star [7.] Square [8.] Circle [9.] Triangle [10.]

crosses. They suggest intensity, activity, keenness and irritation of the qualities shown by the mount or locality where found. On a line, a star is equal to several cuts.

A star on Jupiter indicates social qualities which depend for their acceptance upon genial and kindly deportment, polite attentions and personal presence, appealing to and winning the ideality and emotions.

SQUARES in the hand suggest strength, coolness, regularity, and are, therefore, usually favorable signs. On the mount of Saturn, however, a square will indicate the undue influence of despondency and extreme fear of results. On the mount of Venus, where that is already well developed, it may indicate an undue amount of passion.

CIRCLES on the mounts and phalanges suggest clearness, brilliancy, warmth — and are, therefore, favorable.

On the lines they are, by tradition, unfavorable.

A TRIANGLE indicates an aptitude for actively employing, and putting into effective operation, the peculiar ability suggested by the locality where it occurs.

On the mount of Jupiter it shows success in inventions.

On the mount of Saturn it tells of gloomy forebodings, religious asceticism and fatalism.

On the mount of Apollo, skill in art and success in inventions.

On the mount of Mercury it suggests success in politics, diplomacy and business.

On the mount of Venus it suggests successful love schemes.

On the mount of Mars, ability in an administrative capacity.

On the mount of the Moon happy chastity and mysticism.

CHAPTER VIII.

TYPICAL HANDS.

WHILE hands may be made up of almost any conceivable combination of the different varieties of palms, fingers and thumbs; and while a hand is frequently met with which defies all classification, still, as a general rule, most hands will, more or less clearly, fall into one of the following classes of what may be called "Typical Hands," viz.: Instinctive, Material, Industrious, Progressive, Philosophic, Æsthetic, Intuitive, Psychical.

THE INSTINCTIVE HAND presents a coarse, undeveloped and uninviting aspect. The palm is large, thick and excessively hard; the fingers large, stubbed and ungainly; the nails thick and horny. This hand is the index of dull and slothful senses, ignoble and brutish instincts; of a plodding animalized existence, fitted only for the grosser routine labor of the world. Persons with such hands, when informed at all are usually superstitious, credulous and bigoted. The virtues of such hands are unthinking, dogged obedience; instinctive attachments to home, kindred, and to their superiors; physical courage, kind, habitual persistence. The vices are lack of moral courage, groveling tendencies, brutish living, besotted dissipation, harsh cruelty and selfishness.

I have never met a woman with this hand. The instincts and experiences of maternity are not possible to this type.

This type, with fingers smoother and more pointed, will revel in wild legendary stories, rude poetry, and broad practical jokes, in which personal physical discomfort or annoyance is the principal element.

THE MATERIAL HAND is, in general outline, like an inferior or inelegant æsthetic hand, being more thick and less supple. The fingers are more gross, very little tapering, with spatulate, square, or ill-formed oval tips, and smooth or very moderately undulating. The thumb is above the medium size or large, long and conical. This hand, alike removed from the stolidity of the instinctive and the delicacy of the æsthetic types, exhibits a tendency to material accumulation, avarice, craftiness and sensuality. Riches are its great aim, especially riches in land, shipping, houses, bullion—that is wealth that is tangible and visible, rather than credits, stocks and bonds. This hand suggests hard work for the sake of the earnings; it looks upon labor as a necessary evil with which to overcome the greater evil of poverty. This hand, large and short, opens slowly and shuts tightly; it seizes firmly and holds fast all it grasps. It is more legal than just, more devout than pious. It suggests work, egotism, thrift, avarice; and, in otherwise concurring hands, chicanery, over-reaching, theft, robbery. It is always active, and as other characteristics may control or modify it, is often helpful; frequently connected with a strong, energetic self-reliant, honorable, successful man; even in such case it will suggest the just but exacting dealer, the unsympathetic broker, the close-fisted, hard-faced employer.

The Industrious Hand. — Ascending from the stolidity of the instinctive, and passing the questionable virtues of the material hand, we arrive at the industrious type. This hand is large, thick and strong; hard, firm or elastic. The fingers are well developed, with square or spatulate ends; the knot of material order undulating or large, the first knot slightly undulating or lacking. The thumb is large, especially the first phalange. This hand indexes power rather than delicacy, strength rather than grace, a capacity for muscular endurance, a love of physical activity, self-confidence and persistent application. Persons with this hand desire the material good things of life, and cheerfully toil for comfort and abundance. They study and value practical science. They admire the expenditure of skillful and effective exertion. They work willingly and without undue fatigue, and instead of looking upon labor as a curse, will pray for strength and long days, by which, and in which, to earn, by legitimate labor, its fairest fruits. A man with this hand, if not a laborer — and he will seldom be a mere laborer — will turn his attention to machinery, to field engineering, building, boating, hunting, ball-playing and athletic sports, in which endurance and skill are necessary elements. He will rise early, love fresh air, generous wholesome diet, without many dainties. A similar hand with pointed or oval tips will suggest the horseman or the animal trainer.

This and the next type are especially

common in the anglo-saxon population and among their descendants. The great majority of middle-class Englishmen, and a great preponderance of Americans, will be found in this or the progressive type.

THE PROGRESSIVE HAND is about, or a little above, medium size. The palm is in full proportion, but not excessive, well hollowed and clearly rounded, of fair thickness, and firm or elastic. The fingers are trim and well-shapen, moderately regular, undulating or moderately knotted, and carry clean, square ends — sometimes tending towards the spatulate — or some fingers square and the others spatulate. One wearing this hand will usually be "as regular as clock-work."

"Time is money," says this hand, and, therefore, it values punctuality, continuity, precedent, tradition, law, authority, rule, formality, ceremony — as such. Persons with this hand are proud of their good sense. They have little imagination, little genius and little appreciation or admiration for either, but they possess and worship talent; they are, therefore, most delighted in opposing practice to theory, use to ornament, skill to grace, truth to beauty. In social life they look for moderation, circumspection and prudence; for security and progress. They honor law and authority, but not rank or royalty; and, hence, demand a constitutional and representative government. They are bound by duty, justice and usage, rather than by independent feeling or personal judgment, but will strive to put their ideas into law and usage and live up to them. They depend more upon experience and logic than upon perception and affection, which, however, they regard as vital factors in life. They accept the idea that the world is progressing, and want to accelerate the development, but are conservative in the acceptance of progress in details. They fully appreciate an experiment or a demonstration, and are not only willing but eager to witness the one or listen to the other, and heartily accept the success of either. They are charmed by similitude, conformity, and usage. They are persons of sound practical sense and ability in some one specialty, but usually not profound in general intelligence.

This type in an otherwise weak hand does not, as a general rule, properly value imagination, ideality and general culture. There is a tendency towards heartless calculation and social despotism; also too close an adherence to custom, a disposition to oppose change until it is proven successful; a likelihood of being satisfied with superficial and apparent knowledge and of undervaluing exact and fundamental truth.

This type spatulate will show more self-reliance, more independence of thought, which will recognize the use of law, the power of habit, and the beauty of conformity, but will always act with considerable answer to its individual judgment.

The better this type, the more it approaches the philosophic hand, and then values truths as well as facts.

The Philosophic Hand presents a well developed and elastic palm. The fingers are moderately long, the philosophic knot and the knot of material order are both well defined, and the tips are partly square and partly oval. The thumb is large, the two phalanges of about equal length.

The index finger may be long, tending to a pointed tip, and the first phalange of the thumb may be only moderately developed without changing the type. This variation shows more pride, ideality, invention, and less persistence in study.

The oval tips attest ideality, invention, contemplation, taste, sentiment; the square ends show formalism, medium ideas, comprehensive perception and similitudes; the combination shows originality and sentiment tested by perception and comparison. The well developed knots show capacity for and method in deduction, both ideal and material. The large thumb marks powers of organization, executive ability, and persistent effort to attain the desired result.

The elastic palm shows power of massing the strength into intense effort.

This hand, then, suggests originality, sentiment, perception, calculation, deduction, ability in organization, and power of intense and persistent application; and points out one who duly values exact thinking, and loves essential and universal truths. This hand indicates the inquiring mind that desires "to search out by wisdom concerning all things that are done under heaven;" the mind likely to consider "philosophy as the parent of life, the mother of good deeds and good sayings, the medicine of the mind;" the mind to which reason is more sacred than either instinct, perception or faith, and which, with Socrates, believes that "whatever injures that faculty wounds humanity in its noblest part." This hand brings everything to the test of reason, cultivates logic, inquires the

" why and wherefore," delights in comparison, deduction, demonstration and ratiocination. It entertains no vain scruples, no spiritual terrors, no undue respect for the traditional, customary or mysterious. Instead of being overwhelmed at the vast amount of facts, fancies, and knowledges that are buried in the uncountable books of the world, a person with this hand will rather feel how little certainty there is in the supposed facts recorded; how wild and impossible the fancies, how obscure and indefinite the supposed knowledges; and how few — how very few — the absolutely established truths. A person with this hand, while realizing all this, will still value facts only, or at least mainly, as factors, experience only as evidence, and perceptions as lights for the use of logic in the deduction of truth; and while, as he thinks, duly crediting all these at their full worth, will still believe with Pascal, "that to *think rightly* is the foundation of morality."

THE ÆSTHETIC HAND is characterized by a warm palm, sensitive skin, full mounts of Venus, Jupiter and Apollo, and with shapely, tapering fingers, smooth or very slightly undulating. Among æsthetic hands there are three general sub-classes, each of which appreciates and manifests the beautiful in its own peculiar manner.

The *first* has a flexible palm of moderate size and medium thickness, a small thumb, with the mount of Venus full, clear and firm, indexing impressionability, love of the sublime and grand in form, delight in the pleasures of the senses — the life largely controlled by the sensuous and emotional nature.

The *second* has a short thick hand with a large thumb, indexing richness in combination; less impressionable than the first, but more intelligent and persistent; less diffuse and versatile, but abler in a given direction. The second, like the first, strives after the general and the grand, rather than the particular and the finished. The first will love and express a beautiful object, or scene, or form, regardless of exact truthfulness; while the second will equally love beauty, but desire it to be harmonious with its standard of truth and virtue.

The *third* form of the æsthetic type has a large full palm — highly flexible, elastic or firm; the fingers are long, tapering, and usually full at the third phalanges; the thumb in full proportion to the rest of the hand. This type indexes the love of the beautiful in detail, it suggests elegant finish, love of color, harmony in music, and extreme delight in the sensuous expression and enjoyment of the ideal.

The first proceeds by impression and enthusiasm; the second by perception and delight; the third by the promptings of sensuous pleasure, the love of elegance and finish, and the charm of that realization which at once satisfies the imagination and the senses.

As the æsthetic hand is firm it shows ideality; as it is soft it exhibits impressionability. As the hand and fingers are short there is shown a tendency to the general; as they are long, a love of detail and finish. As the fingers are pointed, they index imagination, without good power of definite expression; as they become square the ability to manipulate is perfected; and when they become spatulate the form or method of expression becomes more material.

Persons with the æsthetic hand will always obey the laws of inspiration, impulse or imagination; they will love the ideal and the sensuous; have a keen dislike for the formal teachings of experience, and the cold severity of deduction; with more or less contempt for the merely useful or productive. They will, with difficulty, conceive of virtue or truth unconnected with beauty — ideal or sensuous. They will fully enter into the spirit of:

"She is beautiful and therefore to be wooed."

They will aspire to paradise, not so much for its purity, as because it is

Beautiful beyond compare,
Bright, rich, radiant and fair.

They may be deaf to the orders of authority, heedless of the claims of duty, unresponsive to the invitations of affection, but they will always be standard bearers where the watchword is

"'Tis beauty calls and glory leads the way."

And, whatever their virtues, misfortunes or faults, they will always feel and sing:

"A thing of beauty is a joy forever."

THE INTUITIVE HAND is, in general outline, like the philosophic hand, except that the former is characterized by medium length or short fingers, quite smooth, gently tapering, with ends square and oval — that is the first and fourth finger tipped in oval or pointed, and the middle and third more square. The size of the thumb does not play as important a part in this type as in the philosophic, and while the second phalange is usually fully developed, the first is often shorter or less full.

This hand, as the name implies, shows one who readily, rapidly and clearly comprehends what is placed before him; who, unlike the philosopher, does not deduce conclusions, but sees them. Persons with such hands see clearly, truthfully, rapidly, fully. They are characteristically perceptive and their first ideas are usually the best. They are not convinced by argument, which may confirm or shake their conclusions, but rarely change them. Additional testimony, a new light thrown upon the subject, an apt illustration, may modify their opinion, but logic, upon them, is wasted.

As this hand is soft and the skin delicate, it shows also impressionability, thus adding warmth and feeling to the clearness, certainty and rapidity of their apprehension of truths and persons, and shows immediate and self-satisfactory conclusion of opinion or plan. It thus verges towards and partakes of the type psychical.

THE PSYCHICAL HAND is the most rare, as it is likewise the most beautiful of hands. It is usually small, always under the medium size. The palm is moderately thick, fairly plump, lithe, supple, soft and highly elastic. The skin is soft without being tender, delicate yet strong; usually of a semi-transparent rosy white; sensitive and invitingly warm. The fingers are smooth and decidedly tapering. The first phalanges are long and oval, or inclined towards the pointed, and carry beautifully outlined, thin, clear, pink nails, with moderate half-moons at their base. The thumb is symmetrical and neither extremely large or small. A thumb less than medium on this hand will show sympathy, desire for companionship, power of persuasion through winning the affections; larger than medium, it will indicate power of will, ability and desire to control, showing ardent, energetic, persistent leadership, which will direct, rather than advise, command rather than argue.

This hand tells of impressionability delicate, distinct, and intense; of feelings warm, earnest and pure; of perceptions clear and satisfactory; of convictions strong and persistent; of aspirations noble, far-reaching and well-defined. It indicates spiritual contemplation — tranquillity or activity, as the other characteristics may determine. It shows poetry of the affections, deep religious sentiment, ardent attachment to a warm ideality, which it will think of as a higher life. It suggests enthusiastic labor, fervid eloquence, and self-denying, unremitting effort for the statement, explanation and spread of the sentiments so strongly and keenly felt, and of the truths so clearly seen. Persons with this hand are religious; but the creed of the philosopher, carefully deduced and logically established, has for them no satisfaction. Neither will the utilitarian views of the industrious or progressive types present to them any charm. The worship of the beautiful by the æsthetic type may please, but will never deeply impress them. The clear seeing of the purely intuitive class, who state the truth in all fullness and clearness, in luminous and precise phraseology, will deeply touch them, and, to some extent, fascinate, with its brilliant charm; but it will still leave an uncultivated void; for the affections are, as yet, unsatisfied. No system of ethics based upon experience, deduced by logic, addressed to the taste simply, or to the intellect only will for long quiet, much less satisfy, those with the true psychical hand. They demand a complete fusion of feeling, thought and action; an affection warm, intense and pure, satisfying the heart; a theology simple, perceptive, harmonious, the natural expression of admitted truths; a charity approved by the conscience; and a morality the natural outgrowth of love for the ideal and of sympathy with the race.

Between such persons and the advancing spiritual tendencies of humanity there is a beautiful and an everlasting affinity.

Whenever great moral or spiritual influences have been exercised in the world, the movement has been begun by those of whom the psychical hand is the index.

The material hand grasps after wealth; the industrious hand extols labor; the progressive hand sings the praises of improvement; the philosopher idolizes essential realities in universal laws, and all these are well in their places, but their places are as followers. The leaders and originators are before them.

The artistic hand sees and admires the beautiful; the intuitive hand recognizes and esteems the true; but the psychical hand sees through the beautiful, into the heart of the true, and there communes with and worships their common soul—the good. The human trinity—like the Divine—is manifested in the Good, the True and the Beautiful; and the greatest of these—the soul, in fact, of the other two—is THE GOOD.

CHAPTER IX.

APPLICATION.

THE character reader must always bear in mind that the hand is considerably changed according to the person's condition. Exact results depend upon close observations and nice discriminations. The true reading of the hand, therefore, will be manifest only when the person is in a normal condition of body and mind.

The attempt to read a hand when first ungloved is usually unsatisfactory. It is then either pale from continued pressure, and consequent lack of blood, or else livid from congestion, occasioned by binding at the wrist or palm. In either case it is somewhat inert from compression of the nerves. It, therefore, requires a little time, after ungloving, for the vital forces to regain their normal control, thus restoring to the hand its natural features and complexion. Neither is the hand of one just waked from sleep a plain page to read; and even more indistinct is the hand of one dull or drowsy from recent overeating, merry or excited from drinking, or much heated from unusual exercise. Quite as indistinct, but in the opposite direction, is the hand of one who is weak from fasting, wearied from exertion, depressed by grief, or exhausted by mental or moral anxieties.

Careful attention, too, must be given to the temperament, complexion, age and physique of the consultant, for in the light of these peculiarities must the hand be interpreted as to its heat, color and general condition.

Each one, after learning the meaning of the details of the hand, must, to a great degree, use his own method in the application of this information. The ability to point out a sign in the hand, and to tell its meaning, does not render one a chiromantist any more than the knowledge of how to spell and define words proves one a journalist or a poet. Knowing the strength of materials, the weight of metals, the cost of labor, and the use of tables and instruments does not entitle one to the name of engineer. It is just as plain that truly recognizing the idiosyncrasies shown by the size, shape and texture of the hand, knowing the meaning of each modification of the fingers, and correctly cataloguing the value of each mount and line, with the ability to read them off in order, does not constitute one a reader of character from the hand. These knowledges are fundamental and indispensable, but it is the power of correct and artistic application that constitutes the psychonomist, who must not only know the value of each element individually, but must also appreciate the comparative value, force and effect of each variable function revealed by the chiromantic peculiarities.

A knowledge of the hand and its meaning simply reveals the elements of the character. Knowing these, the next, and more delicate task, is to feel or see in these elements, and calculate from them, the character associated with them and developed by them.

The method of recognizing, arranging and utilizing such a varied collection of facts and truths, must depend upon the peculiar character of the reader. One with large, long, firm hands and knotted fingers, with square or spatulate ends, must needs pursue a different course from one who has a small, short, soft hand with smooth and pointed fingers.

Not only will the method of application be peculiar to each reader, but the truthfulness of the delineation and the symmetry of the description will be commensurate with his knowledge of the hand, his familiarity with mental and moral law, and his power of construction and statement.

The success of each reader—after knowing the hand, and understanding the value of the factors in development of character—will depend upon delicacy and distinctness of impressionability, clearness and rapidity of perception, power and exactness of logic, facility and thoroughness of combination and the command of precise and perspicuous language. No rule, therefore, is given or even suggested. It could not be followed by any one—not always, even, by the one announcing it. Each reader will naturally fall into a general method peculiar to himself; from which, however, he will frequently deviate as circumstances may determine.

It is appropriate, just here, that the author —who has a medium sized elastic hand, sensitive skin and delicate touch, smooth and slightly undulating fingers, (the logical knots small but clearly defined,) with square and oval ends—should state how he proceeds in delineating a character.

THE AUTHOR'S METHOD.

I sit opposite and facing the consultant, whose two hands, palms upward, I take in mine. As our hands meet I carefully notice any agitation, annoyance, hesitancy or buoyancy of manner. Any such manifestations are significant. They may arise from many different causes, among the more prominent and common of which are the following: Unusual diffidence, modesty, delicacy of feeling, eager desire to learn of self, to know what will be said, simple novelty of the situation, vanity, anxiety to have flattering things said, forward skepticism — real or assumed, superstition, fear — that known faults will be exposed or that sacred matters will be mentioned or discussed. It is frequently a difficult task to determine from what cause or group of causes the agitation arises. At this point I simply note it, to be explained, or at least considered, when summing up the final conclusions, unless it is sooner plainly interpreted. All such agitation, however, must be overcome or allayed — or else due allowance made for it in the reading—without directly alluding to the matter, (which generally makes it worse,) by some common-place questions or remarks.

A glance at the hands gives their size, as compared with the person's body, and also their general shape, showing whether the consultant is one who loves the general or the particular, who analyzes or synthetizes, who thinks or manipulates.

A gentle and careful squeezing tells of their hardness, firmness, elasticity or softness, and thus indicates the degree of physical activity or indolence, and whether the strength is muscular or nervous, material or vital, enduring or intermittent.

The touch, during this squeezing, also announces the quality of the skin, and hence the degree of impressionability, whether the appetites are delicate, sensitive, keen or strong; the temperature of the hand, with the strength and color of the palm and lines, suggest the temperament.

The comparative development of the palm and fingers sets forth the relative power of the sensuous, intellectual or emotional bases of life, and tells whether it is under passional, material, logical or spiritual control. The mount of Venus, and the vital line each imparts information as to the strength, vitality and health, upon each of which so largely depend the direction of effort and the result of action.

The thumb is now questioned as to logic, reason, calculation, applied intelligence, and the first phalange exhibits the power of determination, with the strength and continuity of purpose.

I notice the mounts, and determine which characteristic carries the power of control and the ensign of direction and command.

The comparative length of the fingers, and the peculiarities of their ends — spatulate, square, pointed or mixed — give their testimony; the smooth, undulatory or knotted joints point out intuition, order or logic; and I classify the hand accordingly.

Having now the physical and vital bases, the moving and initiatory powers of passion or emotion, and the guiding elements — material or spiritual, the intellectual idiosyncrasies — inspirational, intuitional or logical, the controlling characteristics (as shown in the fuller mounts), and the incisiveness, strength and continuity of purpose, I am ready to consult and interpret the minutia of the hand in such order as is applicable to the case.

The usual course here is to notice each mount, the fingers as a whole group, then individually, with all the peculiarities of each.

The main lines are then carefully examined in detail, noticing the difference of each one in the right and left hand, and lastly, the accidental lines, in the same manner.

I then make a résumé of the whole, always bearing in mind that the controlling characteristics are the lamps to lighten my way through darkness, conflict or obscurity; remembering that the ruling love:

> "One master passion in the breast,
> Like Aaron's rod, swallows up the rest."

I bear in mind, too, that the good is positive, the bad negative; that the strong is aggressive, the weak only obstructive; that truth is eternal, falsity fleeting; and that, therefore, "the good, the true, and the beautiful" must always achieve success in any honest contest with the evil, the false and the hideous. I keep continually in mind that every physical and mental endowment is for good; that wickedness is the perverted use of good gifts; that vice is the selfish and cowardly surrender of weaknesses to temptations; that those temptations resisted would develop strength; and that temptations overcome transforms innocence into virtue.

I have now as clear and full a knowledge

of the person as I can gain by impressionability and perception, and I turn to the slower and less certain process of deduction. I calculate the force and its direction — passion and control, affection and thought, impulse and intellect, emotion and logic, action and obstacle.

The decision reached, the consultant's character more or less clear in my mind, the next question — and a very important one — is, how much to say. I must, in justice to the consultant, as well as to myself, so far as I say anything, set forth strictly what is obtained by my impressions and perceptions and confirmed by my judgment. The time, place and circumstances, as well as the age, sex, and character of the consultant, must determine much of this. In a mixed company, of the old and young, of both sexes, where there are perhaps strangers, even rivals or enemies, the character must be given in a more subdued key, and painted in a lower light, than in the presence of intimate friends. In any case the surface character, the every-day face given to the public, may be clearly announced. It is, however, only when alone with the consultant, and when there is a mutual confidence, that the endowments most noble and sacred can be reverently pointed out to the fortunate possessor of such treasures. It is only under such conditions that the weaknesses, follies and vices most threatening to the welfare, and most calling for our prayerful pity, can be sorrowfully shown to the afflicted burden-bearer.

This devious route, apparently slow, and somewhat difficult, may, at first glance, seem a labyrinthine maze. With careful study, however, and patient practice, it will unfold to the mind of the faithful student with great rapidity, and will show itself quite orderly and systematic. This method — or any other that the intelligent student may adopt or arrange — will be plain and practical just in the measure that observation, study and experience enable him to feel distinctly, see clearly and think truly.

CONCLUSION.

If some points are still left obscure, others doubtful, and the system itself seems intricate or incomplete, the reader will bear in mind that while

"The proper study of mankind is man,"

it is, also, an infinite and eternal study. He will bear in mind, too, that man, as a machine, simply, is most intricate, delicate and matchless; as a physical being but partially explored, and, hence, but partially known; as an intelligent and thinking individuality but imperfectly and obscurely understood; and as a moral and responsible factor, in the great work of creation and development, only indefinitely and illusively comprehended.

Job asks:

"Canst thou find out the deep things of God,
Or find out the Almighty to perfection?"

Nay, verily, nor can the profoundest philosopher, the grandest seer, or the most inspired prophet — by deduction, perception or revelation — find out to perfection, his humblest fellow-man.

THE END.

SHOW YOUR HAND,

The Chiromantic Album.

This is an elegant quarto volume, designed by the author of "MYSTERIES OF THE HAND," and is intended as a *souvenir* for those who take an interest in "Hand Reading."

This Album is so arranged that each left-hand page affords space for the tracing of a hand, showing its size, shape, character of the fingers,—and in which can be drawn the lines of the palm. The right-hand page is a blank form which when filled out gives a complete description of the hand traced on the opposite page, including the person's autograph.

Each Album contains an appropriate title page, index, full directions for tracing hands and filling the blanks, and space for the tracing and description of "*Fifty Hands.*"

THE CHIROMANTIC ALBUM is beautifully printed upon extra heavy and a superior quality of toned paper, is elegantly and substantially bound, and will be sent to any address, postage prepaid, on receipt of the following prices:

Extra Muslin, Red Edges - - -	2 00
Full Morocco, Gilt Edges - - - -	4 00
Full Russia, Gilt Edges - - -	5 00

J. W. CAMPBELL & CO.,
32 Insurance Exchange,
ST. LOUIS, MO.

www.ingramcontent.com/pod-product-compliance
Lightning Source LLC
Chambersburg PA
CBHW032228230426
43666CB00033B/1633